NORMAN ROCKWELL'S
CHRISTMAS BOOK

NORMAN ROCKWELL'S

MOLLY ROCKWELL *Consulting Editor*

CHRISTMAS BOOK

HARRY N. ABRAMS, INC., Publishers, NEW YORK

Illustrations are of paintings or portions of paintings which appeared in publications by Brown & Bigelow, Inc., Country Gentleman Magazine, Cowles Communications' Look Magazine, Hallmark Cards, Inc., Ladies Home Journal, The Literary Digest, Massachusetts Mutual Life Insurance Company, McCall's Magazine, Parker Pen Co., Inc., The Saturday Evening Post, and The Woman's Home Companion. Illustration on page 174 is from The Adventures of Tom Sawyer © 1936, 1964, The George Macy Companies, Inc., New York.

Special thanks are due to David Wood, Curator, and Margaret Batty, Assistant, of The Old Corner House, Stockbridge, Massachusetts, for their cooperation, and to Hallmark Cards, Inc., for theirs.

Project editor, Lena Tabori Fried

Editor, Ruth Eisenstein

Designer, Julie Bergen

Director Rights and Reproductions, Barbara Lyons

Library of Congress Cataloging in Publication Data

Main entry under title:
Norman Rockwell's Christmas book.

SUMMARY: Stories, poems, carols, and recollections of Christmas by world-famous authors, with 120 illustrations by Norman Rockwell.
1. Christmas—Literary collection. [1. Christmas—Literary collections] I. Rockwell, Norman, 1894-
II. Rockwell, Molly.
PZ5.N59   [Fic]   77-7087
ISBN 0-7917-1261-3

Library of Congress Catalogue Card Number: 77-7087
This is a reprint edition distributed by Bookthrift, New York.

Printed in Hong Kong

ACKNOWLEDGMENTS

"Well, so that is that" from "The Flight into Egypt" by W. H. Auden. Copyright 1944 by W. H. Auden. Reprinted from *Collected Poems*, edited by Edward Mendelson, by permission of Random House, Inc.

"My Christmas Miracle" by Taylor Caldwell. Reprinted by permission of *Family Weekly*, copyright © 1968, 641 Lexington Avenue, New York, New York 10022.

"Christmas in Maine" by Robert P. Tristram Coffin. Copyright 1941 by R. P. T. Coffin. Renewed 1968 by R. P. T. Coffin, Jr.

"Christmas on a Farm in New York" by Theodore Ledyard Cuyler. Reprinted from *The Twelve Days of Christmas* by Miles and John Hadfield. Copyright 1961 by Little, Brown and Company, Boston.

"Mistletoe" by Walter de la Mare. Reprinted by permission of The Literary Trustees of Walter de la Mare, and The Society of Authors, London.

"Our Lady's Juggler" by Anatole France. Reprinted from *Mother of Pearl*, published by Dodd, Mead and Company.

"Christmas Trees" by Robert Frost. From *The Poetry of Robert Frost* edited by Edward Connery Lathem. Copyright 1916, © 1969 by Holt, Rinehart and Winston. Copyright 1944 by Robert Frost. Reprinted by permission of Holt, Rinehart and Winston, Publishers.

"The Miraculous Staircase" by Arthur Gordon. Reprinted by permission from *Guideposts Magazine*, copyright December 1966 by Guideposts Associates, Inc., Carmel, New York 10512.

"The Gift of the Magi" by O. Henry. Reprinted from *The Four Million*, published by Doubleday and Company, Inc.

"One Christmas Eve" by Langston Hughes. From *The Ways of White Folks* by Langston Hughes. Copyright 1934 and renewed 1962 by Langston Hughes. Reprinted by permission of Alfred A. Knopf, Inc.

"Legend of the Christmas Rose" by Selma Lagerlöf. From *The Girl from Marsh Croft* by S. Lagerlöf. Copyright 1910 by S. Lagerlöf. Reprinted by permission of Doubleday and Company, Inc.

"A Surprise for the Teacher" by Sam Levenson. From *Christmas with Ed Sullivan* by Ed Sullivan. Copyright © 1959 by Ed Sullivan. Used with permission of McGraw-Hill Book Company.

"Christmas Eve at Sea" by John Masefield. From *Salt-Water Poems and Ballads* by John Masefield. Copyright 1916 by John Masefield, renewed 1944 by John Masefield. Reprinted by permission of Macmillan.

"Christmas Eve in Our Village" by Phyllis McGinley. From *Times Three* by Phyllis McGinley. Copyright 1951 by Phyllis McGinley. First published in *The New Yorker*. Reprinted by permission of The Viking Press.

"The Worst Christmas Story" by Christopher Morley. From *Letters of Askance*, by Christopher Morley. Copyright 1939 by Christopher Morley. Reprinted by permission of J. B. Lippincott Company.

"A Carol for Children" by Ogden Nash. Copyright 1934 by Ogden Nash.

"The Boy Who Laughed at Santa Claus" by Ogden Nash. Copyright 1937 by Ogden Nash.

"A Gift of the Heart" by Norman Vincent Peale. Reprinted with permission from the January 1968 *Reader's Digest*. Copyright 1968 by The Reader's Digest Association, Inc.

"Down Pens" by Saki. From *The Short Stories of Saki* (H. H. Munro). All rights reserved. Reprinted by permission of The Viking Press.

"A Miserable, Merry Christmas" by Lincoln Steffens. From *The Autobiography of Lincoln Steffens*, copyright 1931 by Harcourt Brace Jovanovich, Inc.; renewed 1959 by Peter Steffens. Reprinted by permission of the publishers.

"Christmas This Year" by Booth Tarkington. Privately printed by Booth Tarkington, 1945.

"Once on Christmas" by Dorothy Thompson. Copyright 1938 by Oxford University Press. Renewed 1966 by Michael Lewis.

"Letter from Santa Claus" by Mark Twain. Pages 36–39 in *My Father Mark Twain* by Clara Clemens. Copyright 1931 by Clara Clemens Gabrilowitsch; renewed 1931 by Clara Clemens Samossoud. Reprinted by permission of Harper and Row, Publishers, Inc.

"Mr. Edwards Meets Santa Claus" by Laura Ingalls Wilder. From *Little House on the Prairie*, by Laura Ingalls Wilder. Text copyright by Laura Ingalls Wilder. © renewed 1963 by Roger L. MacBride. Reprinted by permission of Harper and Row, Publishers, Inc.

Fifteen songs and carols from *A Treasury of Christmas Songs and Carols* edited and annotated by Henry W. Simon. By permission of Barthold Fles, Literary Agent, New York.

CONTENTS

THE FIRST CHRISTMAS

STORIES

CAROLS

POEMS

CHRISTMAS REMEMBERED

A
LIST OF
AUTHORS

LOUISA MAY AL-
COTT (1832–1888) • HANS
CHRISTIAN ANDERSEN
(1805–1875) • W.H. AUDEN (1907–
1973) • TAYLOR CALDWELL (b. 1900) •
LEWIS CARROLL
(CHARLES LUTWIDGE
DODGSON; 1832–1898) •
FRANCIS P. CHURCH (1839–
1906) • JOHN CLARE (1793–1864) •
ROBERT P. TRISTRAM COFFIN (1892–
1955) • RICHARD CRASHAW (1613–1649) •
THEODORE LEDYARD CUYLER (1822–1909) •
WALTER DE LA MARE (1873–1956) • CHARLES DICK-
ENS (1812–1870) • FANNIE MERRITT FARMER (1857–1915)
• ANATOLE FRANCE (1844–1924) • ROBERT FROST (1874–
1963) • ARTHUR GORDON (b. 1912) • O. HENRY (WILLIAM
SIDNEY PORTER; 1862–1910) • ROBERT HERRICK (1591–1674) •
WILLIAM DEAN HOWELLS (1837–
1920) • LANGSTON HUGHES (1902–
1967) • SELMA LAGERLÖF (1858–1940) •
SAM LEVENSON (b. 1911) • GEORGE MAC-
DONALD (1824–1905) • PHYLLIS McGINLEY
(b. 1905) • JOHN MASEFIELD (1878–1967) • JOHN
MILTON (1608–1674) • CLEMENT CLARKE MOORE
(1779–1863) • CHRISTOPHER MORLEY (1890–1957) • ELIZ-
ABETH MORROW (1873–1955) • OGDEN NASH (1902–1971) •
NORMAN VINCENT PEALE (b. 1898) • SAKI (H.H. MUNRO;
1870–1916) • WILLIAM SHAKESPEARE (1564–1616) • CHRISTO-
PHER SMART (1722–1771) • LINCOLN STEFFENS (1866–1936) • BOOTH
TARKINGTON (1869–1946) • WILLIAM MAKEPEACE THACKERAY (1811–
1863) • DOROTHY THOMPSON (1894–1961) • MARK TWAIN (SAMUEL
LANGHORNE CLEMENS; 1835–1910) • LAURA INGALLS WILDER (1867–1957)

THE FIRST CHRISTMAS

Born in Bethlehem

(ST. LUKE 2:1–16)

And it came to pass in those days, that there went out a decree from Caesar Augustus, that all the world should be taxed.

(*And* this taxing was first made when Cyrenius was governor of Syria.)

And all went to be taxed, every one into his own city.

And Joseph also went up from Galilee, out of the city of Nazareth, into Judæa, unto the city of David, which is called Bethlehem; (because he was of the house and lineage of David:)

To be taxed with Mary his espoused wife, being great with child.

And so it was, that, while they were there, the days were accomplished that she should be delivered.

And she brought forth her firstborn son, and wrapped him in swaddling clothes, and laid him in a manger; because there was no room for them in the inn.

And there were in the same country shepherds abiding in the field, keeping watch over their flock by night.

And, lo, the angel of the Lord came upon them, and the glory of the Lord shone round about them: and they were sore afraid.

And the angel said unto them, Fear not: for, behold, I bring you good tidings of great joy, which shall be to all people.

For unto you is born this day in the city of David a Saviour, which is Christ the Lord.

And this *shall be* a sign unto you; Ye shall find the babe wrapped in swaddling clothes, lying in a manger.

And suddenly there was with the angel a multitude of the heavenly host praising God, and saying,

Glory to God in the highest, and on earth peace, good will toward men.

And it came to pass, as the angels were gone away from them into heaven, the shepherds said one to another, Let us now go even unto Bethlehem, and see this thing which is come to pass, which the Lord hath made known unto us.

And they came with haste, and found Mary, and Joseph, and the babe lying in a manger.

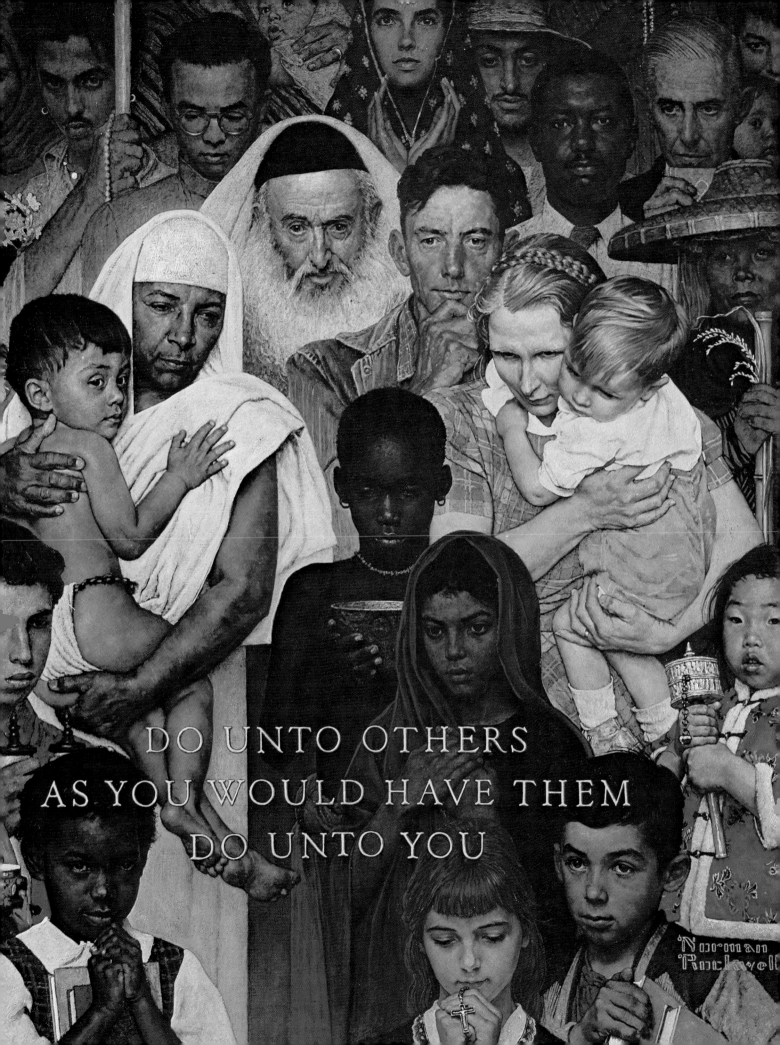

The Three Wise Men

(ST. MATTHEW 2:1–14)

Now when Jesus was born in Bethlehem of Judæa in the days of Herod the king, behold, there came wise men from the east to Jerusalem.

Saying, Where is he that is born King of the Jews? for we have seen his star in the east, and are come to worship him.

When Herod the king had heard *these things*, he was troubled, and all Jerusalem with him.

And when he had gathered all the chief priests and scribes of the people together, he demanded of them where Christ should be born.

And they said unto him, In Bethlehem of Judæa: for thus it is written by the prophet,

And thou Bethlehem, *in* the land of Juda, art not the least among the princes of Juda: for out of thee shall come a Governor, that shall rule my people Israel.

Then Herod, when he had privily called the wise men, enquired of them diligently what time the star appeared.

And he sent them to Bethlehem, and said, Go and search diligently for the young child; and when ye have found *him*, bring me word again, that I may come and worship him also.

When they had heard the king, they departed; and, lo, the star, which they saw in the east, went before them, till it came and stood over where the young child was.

When they saw the star, they rejoiced with exceeding great joy.

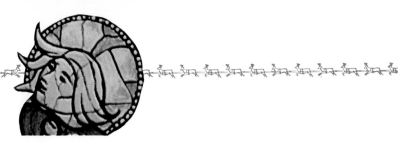

And when they were come into the house, they saw the young child with Mary his mother, and fell down, and worshipped him: and when they had opened their treasures, they presented unto him gifts; gold, and frankincense, and myrrh.

And being warned of God in a dream that they should not return to Herod, they departed into their own country another way.

And when they were departed, behold, the angel of the Lord appeareth to Joseph in a dream, saying, Arise, and take the young child and his mother, and flee into Egypt, and be thou there until I bring thee word: for Herod will seek the young child to destroy him.

When he arose, he took the young child and his mother by night, and departed into Egypt.

The Cherry Tree Carol

Joseph was an old man,
    and an old man was he,
When he wedded Mary,
    in the land of Galilee.

Joseph and Mary walked
    through an orchard good,
Where was cherries and berries,
    so red as any blood.

Joseph and Mary walked
    through an orchard green,
Where was berries and cherries,
    as thick as might be seen.

O then bespoke Mary,
    so meek and so mild:
'Pluck me one cherry, Joseph,
    for I am with child.'

O then bespoke Joseph,
   with words most unkind:
'Let him pluck thee a cherry
   that brought thee with child.'

O then bespoke the babe
   within his mother's womb;
'Bow down then the tallest tree,
   for my mother to have some.'

Then bowed down the highest tree
   unto his mother's hand;
Then she cried, 'See, Joseph,
   I have cherries at command.'

O then bespoke Joseph:
   'I have done Mary wrong;
But cheer up, my dearest,
   and be not cast down.'

Then Mary plucked a cherry,
   as red as the blood,
Then Mary went home
   With her heavy load.

Then Mary took her babe,
   and sat him on her knee,
Saying, 'My dear son, tell me,
   what this world will be.'

'O I shall be as dead, mother,
   as the stones in the wall;
O the stones in the streets, mother,
   shall mourn for me all.

'Upon Easter day, mother,
   my uprising shall be;
O the sun and the moon, mother,
   shall both rise with me.'

Some say…

WILLIAM SHAKESPEARE

Some say that ever 'gainst that season comes
Wherein our Saviour's birth is celebrated,
The bird of dawning singeth all night long:
And then, they say, no spirit dare stir abroad,
The nights are wholesome, then no planets strike,
No fairy takes nor witch hath power to charm,
So hallow'd and so gracious is the time.

—*Hamlet*, Act 1, Scene 1

The Nativity of Our Lord and Saviour Jesus Christ

CHRISTOPHER SMART

Where is this stupendous stranger,
   Swains of Solyma, advise,
Lead me to my Master's manger,
   Shew me where my Saviour lies?...

Nature's decorations glisten
   Far above their usual trim;
Birds on box and laurel listen,
   As so near the cherubs hymn.

Boreas now no longer winters
   On the desolated coast;
Oaks no more are riv'n in splinters
   By the whirlwind and his host.

Spinks and ouzels sing sublimely,
   "We too have a Saviour born";
Whiter blossoms burst untimely
   On the blest Mosaic thorn.

God all-bounteous, all-creative,
   Whom no ills from good dissuade,
Is incarnate, and a native
   Of the very world he made.

A Hymn Sung as by
the Shepherds

RICHARD CRASHAW

Welcome, all wonders in one sight!
Eternity shut in a span!
    Summer in winter, day in night!
Heaven in earth, and God in man!
    Great little One! whose all-embracing birth
Lifts earth to heaven, stoops heaven to earth. . . .
                . . .
    To Thee, meek Majesty! soft King
Of simple graces and sweet loves:
    Each of us his lamb will bring,
Each his pair of silver doves;
    Till burnt at last in fire of Thy fair eyes,
Ourselves become our own best sacrifice.

That Holy Thing

GEORGE MacDONALD

They all were looking for a king
   To slay their foes and lift them high:
Thou cam'st, a little baby thing
   That made a woman cry.

O Son of Man, to right my lot
   Naught but Thy presence can avail;
Yet on the road Thy wheels are not,
   Nor on the sea Thy sail!

My how or when Thou wilt not heed,
   But come down Thine own secret stair,
That Thou mayst answer all my need—
   Yea, every bygone prayer.

On the Morning of Christ's Nativity

JOHN MILTON

Say, Heavenly Muse, shall not thy sacred vein
Afford a present to the Infant God?
Hast thou no verse, no hymn, or solemn strain,
To welcome him to this his new abode,
Now while the heaven, by the sun's team untrod,
　　Hath took no print of the approaching light,
And all the spangled host keep watch in squadrons bright?

See how from far upon the eastern road
The star-led wizards haste with odours sweet!
O run; prevent them with thy humble ode,
And lay it lowly at his blessed feet;
Have thou the honour first thy Lord to greet
　　And join thy voice unto the angel quire,
From out his secret altar touched with hallowed fire.

The Hymn

It was the winter wild,
While the Heaven-born Child
　　All meanly wrapt in the rude manger lies;
Nature in awe to him
Had doffed her gaudy trim,
　　With her great Master so to sympathize:
It was no season then for her
To wanton with the sun, her lusty paramour.
　　　　. . .
But he, her fears to cease,
Sent down the meek-eyed Peace;
　　She crowned with olive green came softly sliding
Down through the turning sphere,
His ready harbinger,
　　With turtle wing the amorous clouds dividing,
And waving wide her myrtle wand,
She strikes a universal peace through sea and land.
　　　　. . .

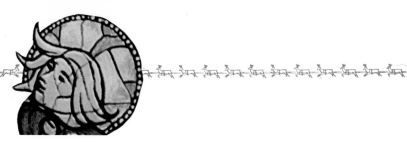

The stars, with deep amaze,
Stand fixed in steadfast gaze,
   Bending one way their precious influence,
And will not take their flight,
For all the morning light,
   Or Lucifer that often warned them thence;
But in their glimmering orbs did glow,
Until their Lord himself bespake, and bid them go.
. . .

The shepherds on the lawn,
Or ere the point of dawn,
   Sat simply chatting in a rustic row;
Full little thought they then
That the mighty Pan
   Was kindly come to live with them below;
Perhaps their loves or else their sheep,
Was all that did their silly thoughts so busy keep.

. . .

When such music sweet
Their hearts and ears did greet,
   As never was by mortal finger strook,
Divinely warbled voice
Answering the stringèd noise
   As all their souls in blissful rapture took:
The air such pleasure loth to lose,
With thousand echoes still prolongs each heavenly close.

. . .

But see! the Virgin blest
Hath laid her Babe to rest.
   Time is our tedious song should here have ending:
Heaven's youngest-teemèd star
Hath fixed her polished car,
   Her sleeping Lord with handmaid lamp attending;
And all about the courtly stable
Bright-harnessed angels sit in order serviceable.

A Carol for Children

OGDEN NASH

God rest you merry, Innocents,
Let nothing you dismay,
Let nothing wound an eager heart
Upon this Christmas day.

Yours be the genial holly wreaths,
The stockings and the tree;
An aged world to you bequeaths
Its own forgotten glee.

Soon, soon enough come crueler gifts,
The anger and the tears;
Between you now there sparsely drifts
A handful yet of years.

Oh, dimly, dimly glows the star
Through the electric throng;
The bidding in temple and bazaar
Drowns out the silver song.

The ancient altars smoke afresh,
The ancient idols stir;
Faint in the reek of burning flesh
Sink frankincense and myrrh.

Gaspar, Balthazar, Melchior!
Where are your offerings now?
What greetings to the Prince of War,
His darkly branded brow?

Two ultimate laws alone we know,
The ledger and the sword—
So far away, so long ago,
We lost the infant Lord.

Only the children clasp His hand;
His voice speaks low to them,
And still for them the shining band
Wings over Bethlehem.

God rest you merry, Innocents,
While Innocence endures.
A sweeter Christmas than we to ours
May you bequeath to yours.

STORIES

The Fir Tree

HANS CHRISTIAN ANDERSEN

Out in the forest stood a pretty little Fir Tree. It had a good place; it could have sunlight, air there was in plenty, and all around grew many larger comrades—pines as well as firs. But the little Fir Tree wished ardently to become greater. It did not care for the warm sun and the fresh air; it took no notice of the peasant children, who went about talking together, when they had come out to look for strawberries and raspberries. Often they came with a whole potful, or had strung berries on a straw; then they would sit down by the little Fir Tree and say, "How pretty and small that one is!" and the Fir Tree did not like to hear that at all.

Next year he had grown a great joint, and the following year he was longer still, for in fir trees one can always tell by the number of rings they have how many years they have been growing.

"Oh, if I were only as great a tree as the others!" sighed the little Fir, "then I would spread my branches far around and look out from my crown into the wide world. The birds would then build nests in my boughs, and when the wind blew I could nod just as grandly as the others yonder."

He took no pleasure in the sunshine, in the birds, and in the red clouds that went sailing over him morning and evening.

When it was winter, the snow lay all around, white and sparkling, a hare would often come jumping along, and spring right over the little Fir Tree. Oh! this made him so angry. But two winters went by, and when the third came the little Tree had grown so tall that the hare was obliged to run around it.

"Oh! to grow, to grow, and become old; that's the only fine thing in the world," thought the Tree.

In the autumn woodcutters always came and felled a few of the largest trees; that was done this year too, and the little Fir Tree, that was now quite well grown, shuddered with fear, for the great stately trees fell to the ground with a crash, and their branches were cut off, so that the trees looked quite naked, long, and slender—they could hardly be recognized. But then they were laid upon wagons, and horses dragged them away out of the wood. Where were they going? What destiny awaited them?

In the spring when the Swallows and the Stork came, the Tree asked them, "Do you know where they were taken? Did you not meet them?"

The Swallows knew nothing about it, but the Stork looked thoughtful, nodded his head, and said:

"Yes, I think so. I met many new ships when I flew out of Egypt; on the ships were stately masts; I fancy these were the trees. They smelled like fir. I can assure you they're stately—very stately."

"Oh that I were only big enough to go over the sea! What kind of thing is this sea, and how does it look?"

"It would take too long to explain all that," said the Stork, and he went away.

"Rejoice in thy youth," said the Sunbeams; "rejoice in thy fresh growth, and in the young life that is within thee."

And the wind kissed the Tree, and the dew wept tears upon it; but the Fir Tree did not understand about that.

When Christmas time approached, quite young trees were felled, sometimes trees which were neither so old nor so large as this Fir Tree, that never rested, but always wanted to go away. These young trees, which were always the most beautiful, kept all their branches; they were put upon wagons, and the horses dragged them away out of the wood.

·"Where are they all going?" asked the Fir Tree. "They are not greater than I—indeed, one of them was much smaller. Why do they keep all their branches? Whither are they taken?"

"We know that! We know that!" chirped the Sparrows. "Yonder in the town we looked in at the windows. We know where they go. Oh! they are dressed up in the greatest pomp and splendor that can be imagined. We have looked in at the windows, and have perceived that they are planted in the middle of a warm room, and adorned with the most beautiful things—gilt apples, honey cakes, playthings, and many hundreds of candles."

"And then?" asked the Fir Tree, and trembled through all its branches. "And then? What happens then?"

"Why, we have not seen anything more. But it is incomparable."

"Perhaps I may be destined to tread this glorious path one day!" cried the Fir Tree, rejoicingly. "That is even better than traveling across the sea. How painfully I long for it! If it were only Christmas now! Now I am great and grown up, like the rest who were led away last year. Oh, if I were only on the carriage! If I were only in the warm room, among all the pomp and splendor! And then? Yes, then something even better will come, something far more charming, or else why should they adorn me so? There must be something grander, something greater still to come; but what? Oh! I'm suffering. I'm longing! I don't know myself what is the matter with me!"

"Rejoice in us," said the Air and Sunshine. "Rejoice in thy fresh youth here in the woodland."

But the Fir Tree did not rejoice at all, but it grew and grew; winter and summer it stood there, green, dark green. The people who saw it said, "That's a handsome tree!" and at Christmas time it was felled before any of the others. The ax cut deep into its marrow, and the tree fell to the ground with a sigh; it felt a pain, a sensation of faintness, and could not think at all of happiness, for it was sad at parting from its home, from the place where it had grown up; it knew that it should never again see the dear old companions, the little bushes and flowers all around—perhaps not even the birds. The parting was not at all agreeable.

The Tree only came to itself when it was unloaded in a yard, with other trees, and heard a man say:

"This one is famous; we want only this one!"

Now two servants came in gay liveries, and carried the Fir Tree into a large, beautiful salon. All around the walls hung pictures, and by the great stove stood large Chinese vases with lions on the covers; there were rocking-chairs, silken sofas, great tables covered with picture-books, and toys worth a hundred times a hundred dollars, at least the children said so. And the Fir Tree was put into a great tub filled with sand; but no one could see that it was a tub, for it was hung round with green cloth, and stood on a large, many-colored carpet. Oh, how the Tree trembled! What was to happen now? The servants, and the young ladies also, decked it out. On one branch they hung little nets, cut out of colored paper; every net was filled with sweetmeats; golden apples and walnuts hung down, as if they grew there, and more than a hundred little candles, red, white, and blue, were fastened to the different boughs. Dolls that looked exactly like real people—the tree had never seen such before—swung among the foliage, and high on the summit of the Tree was fixed a tinsel star. It was splendid, particularly splendid.

"This evening," said all, "this evening it will shine."

"Oh," thought the Tree, "that it were evening already! Oh, that the lights may soon be lit up!

When may that be done? Will the sparrows fly against the panes? Shall I grow fast here, and stand adorned in summer and winter?"

Yes, he did not guess badly. But he had a complete backache from mere longing, and backache is just as bad for a tree as a headache for a person.

At last the candles were lighted. What a brilliance, what a splendor! The Tree trembled so in all its branches that one of the candles set fire to a green twig, and it was scorched.

"Heaven preserve us!" cried the young ladies; and they hastily put the fire out.

Now the Tree might not even tremble. Oh, that was terrible! It was so afraid of setting fire to some of its ornaments, and it was quite bewildered with all the brilliance. And now the folding doors were thrown wide open, and a number of children rushed in as if they would have overturned the whole Tree; the older people followed more deliberately. The little ones stood quite silent, but only for a minute; then they shouted till the room rang; they danced gleefully round the Tree, and one present after another was plucked from it.

"What are they about?" thought the Tree. "What's going to be done?"

And the candles burned down to the twigs, and as they burned down they were extinguished, and then the children received permission to plunder the Tree. Oh! they rushed in upon it, so that every branch cracked again: if it had not been fastened by the top and by the golden star to the ceiling, it would have fallen down.

The children danced about with their pretty toys. No one looked at the Tree except one old man, who came up and peeped among the branches, but only to see if a fig or an apple had not been forgotten.

"A story! A story!" shouted the children; and they drew a little fat man toward the tree; and he sat down just beneath it—"for then we shall be in the green wood," said he, "and the tree may have the advantage of listening to my tale. But I can only tell one. Will you hear the story of Ivede-Avede, or of Klumpey-Dumpey, who fell downstairs, and still was raised up to honor and married the Princess?"

"Ivede-Avede!" cried some, "Klumpey-Dumpey!" cried others, and there was a great crying and shouting. Only the Fir Tree was quite silent, and thought, "Shall I not be in it? Shall I have nothing to do in it?" But he had been in the evening's amusement, and had done what was required of him.

And the fat man told about Klumpey-Dumpey who fell downstairs and yet was raised to honor and married a Princess. And the children clapped their hands and cried, "Tell another! tell another!" and they wanted to hear about Ivede-Avede; but they only got the story of Klumpey-Dumpey. The Fir Tree stood quite silent and thoughtful; never had the birds in the wood told such a story as that. Klumpey-Dumpey fell downstairs, and yet came to honor and married a Princess!

"Yes, so it happens in the world!" thought the Fir Tree, and believed it must be true, because that was such a nice man who told it.

"Well, who can know? Perhaps I shall fall downstairs, too, and marry a Princess!" And it looked forward with pleasure to being adorned again, the next evening, with candles and toys, gold and fruit. "Tomorrow I shall not tremble," it thought.

"I shall rejoice in all my splendor. Tomorrow I shall hear the story of Klumpey-Dumpey again, and perhaps that of Ivede-Avede, too."

And the Tree stood all night quiet and thoughtful.

In the morning the servants and the chambermaid came in.

"Now my splendor will begin afresh," thought the Tree. But they dragged him out of the room, and upstairs to the garret, and here they put him in a dark corner where no daylight shone.

"What's the meaning of this?" thought the Tree. "What am I to do here? What is to happen?"

And he leaned against the wall, and thought,

and thought. And he had time enough, for days and nights went by, and nobody came up; and when at length some one came, it was only to put some great boxes in a corner. Now the Tree stood quite hidden away, and the supposition is that it was quite forgotten.

"Now it's winter outside," thought the Tree. "The earth is hard and covered with snow, and people cannot plant me; therefore I suppose I'm to be sheltered here until Spring comes. How considerate that is! How good people are! If it were only not so dark here, and so terribly solitary!—not even a little hare? That was pretty out there in the wood, when the snow lay thick and the hare sprang past; yes, even when he jumped over me; but then I did not like it. It is terribly lonely up here!"

"Piep! piep!" said a little Mouse, and crept forward, and then came another little one. They smelled at the Fir Tree, and then slipped among the branches.

"It's horribly cold," said the two little Mice, "or else it would be comfortable here. Don't you think so, old Fir Tree?"

"I'm not old at all," said the Fir Tree. "There are many much older than I."

"Where do you come from?" asked the Mice. "And what do you know?" They were dreadfully inquisitive. "Tell us about the most beautiful spot on earth. Have you been there? Have you been in the storeroom, where cheeses lie on the shelves, and hams hang from the ceiling, where one

dances on tallow candles, and goes in thin and comes out fat?"

"I don't know that," replied the Tree; "but I know the wood, where the sun shines and the birds sing."

And then it told all about its youth.

And the little Mice had never heard anything of the kind; and they listened and said:

"What a number of things you have seen! How happy you must have been!"

"I?" replied the Fir Tree; and it thought about what it had told. "Yes, those were really quite happy times." But then he told of the Christmas Eve, when he had been hung with sweetmeats and candles.

"Oh!" said the little Mice, "how happy you have been, you old Fir Tree!"

"I'm not old at all," said the Tree. "I only came out of the wood this winter. I'm only rather backward in my growth."

"What splendid stories you can tell!" said the little Mice.

And the next night they came with four other little Mice, to hear what the Tree had to relate; and the more it said, the more clearly did it remember everything, and thought. "Those were quite merry days! But they may come again. Klumpey-Dumpey fell downstairs, and yet he married a Princess. Perhaps I shall marry a Princess, too!" And the Fir Tree thought of a pretty little Birch Tree that grew out in the forest; for the Fir Tree, that Birch was a real Princess.

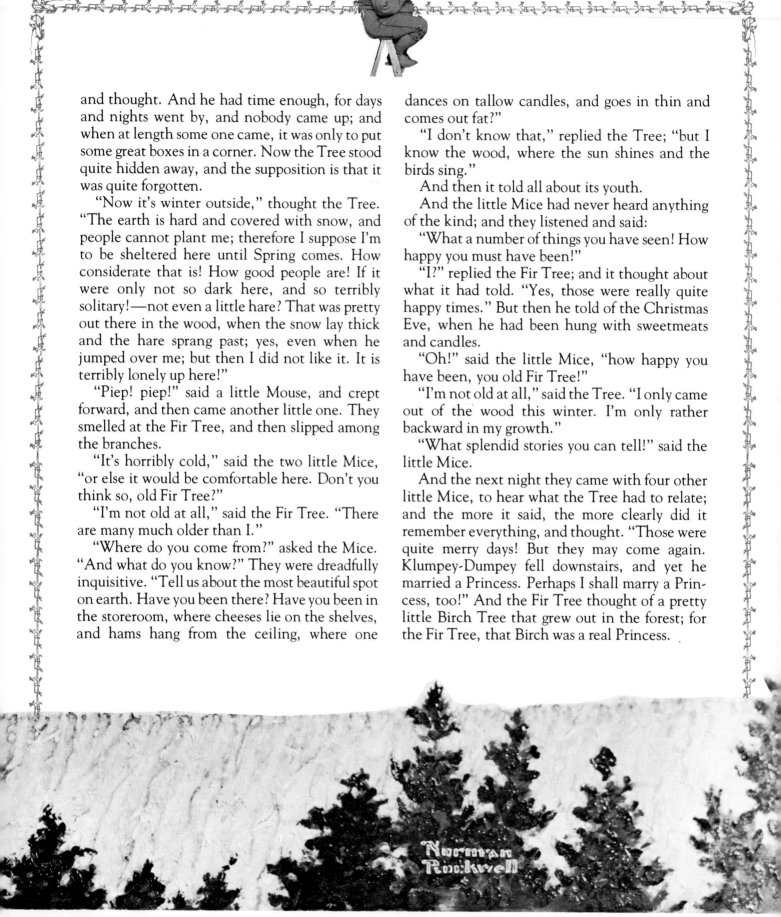

"Who's Klumpey-Dumpey?" asked the little Mice.

And then the Fir Tree told the whole story. It could remember every single word; and the little Mice were ready to leap to the very top of the Tree with pleasure. Next night a great many more Mice came, and on Sunday two Rats even appeared; but these thought the story was not pretty, and the little Mice were sorry for that, for now they also did not like it so much as before.

"Do you know only one story?" asked the Rats.

"Only that one," replied the Tree. "I heard that on the happiest evening of my life; I did not think then how happy I was."

"That's a very miserable story. Don't you know any about bacon and tallow candles—a storeroom story?"

"No," said the Tree.

"Then we'd rather not hear you," said the Rats.

And they went back to their own people. The little Mice at last stayed away also; and then the Tree sighed and said:

"It was very nice when they sat round me, the merry little Mice, and listened when I spoke to them. Now that's past too. But I shall remember to be pleased when they take me out."

But when did that happen? Why, it was one morning that people came and rummaged in the garret; the boxes were put away, and the tree brought out; they certainly threw him rather roughly on the floor, but a servant dragged him away at once to the stairs, where the daylight shone.

"Now life is beginning again!" thought the Tree.

It felt the fresh air and the first sunbeam, and now it was out in the courtyard. Everything passed so quickly that the Tree quite forgot to look at itself, there was so much to look at all round. The courtyard was close to a garden, and here everything was blooming; the roses hung fresh over the paling, the linden trees were in blossom, and the swallows cried, "Quinze-wit! quinze-wit! my husband's come!" But it was not the Fir Tree they meant.

"Now I shall live!" said the Tree, rejoicingly, and spread its branches far out; but, alas! they were all withered and yellow; and it lay in the corner among nettles and weeds. The tinsel star was still upon it, and shone in the bright sunshine.

In the courtyard a couple of the merry children were playing who had danced round the tree at Christmas time, and had rejoiced over it. One of the youngest ran up and tore off the golden star.

"Look what is sticking to the ugly old fir tree!" said the child, and he trod upon the branches till they cracked again under his boots.

And the Tree looked at all the blooming flowers and the splendor of the garden, and then looked at itself, and wished it had remained in the dark corner of the garret; it thought of its fresh youth in the wood, of the merry Christmas Eve, and of the little Mice which had listened so pleasantly to the story of Klumpey-Dumpey.

"Past! past!" said the old Tree. "Had I but rejoiced when I could have done so! Past! past!"

And the servant came and chopped the Tree into little pieces; a whole bundle lay there; it blazed brightly under the great brewing copper, and it sighed deeply, and each sigh was like a little shot; and the children who were at play there ran up and seated themselves at the fire, looked into it, and cried "Puff! puff!" But at each explosion, which was a deep sigh, the Tree thought of a summer day in the woods, or of a winter night there, when the stars beamed; he thought of Christmas Eve and of Klumpey-Dumpey, the only story he had ever heard or knew how to tell; and then the Tree was burned.

The boys played in the garden, and the youngest had on his breast a golden star, which the Tree had worn on its happiest evening. Now that was past, and the Tree's life was past, and the story is past too: past! past!—and that's the way with all stories.

A Pint of Judgment

ELIZABETH MORROW

The Tucker family made out lists of what they wanted for Christmas. They did not trust to Santa Claus' taste or the wisdom of aunts and uncles in such an important matter. By the first week in December everybody had written out what he or she hoped to receive.

Sally, who was seven, when she could only print had sent little slips of paper up the chimney with her desires plainly set forth. She had wondered sometimes if neatly written requests like Ellen's were not more effective than the printed ones. Ellen was eight. She had asked last year for a muff and Santa had sent it.

Mother always explained that one should not expect to get all the things on the list; "Only what you want most, dear, and sometimes you have to wait till you are older for those."

For several years Sally had asked for a lamb and she had almost given up hope of finding one tied to her stocking on Christmas morning. She had also asked for a white cat and a dove and they had not come either. Instead a bowl of goldfish had been received. Now she wrote so plainly that there was no excuse for misunderstandings like this.

Derek still printed his list—he was only six and yet he had received an Indian suit the very first time he asked for it. It was puzzling.

Caroline, called "Lovey" for short, just stood on the hearth rug and shouted "Dolly! Bow wow!" but anybody with Santa Claus' experience would know that rag dolls and woolly dogs were the proper presents for a four-year-old.

The lists were useful too in helping one to decide what to make for Father and Mother and

the others for Christmas. The little Tuckers had been brought up by their grandmother in the belief that a present you made yourself was far superior to one bought in a store. Mother always asked for a great many things the children could make. She was always wanting knitted washcloths, pincushion covers, blotters, and penwipers. Father needed pipe cleaners, calendars and decorated match boxes.

This year Sally longed to do something quite different for her mother. She was very envious of Ellen, who had started a small towel as her present, and was pulling threads for a fringed end.

"Oh! Ellen! How lovely that is!" she sighed. "It is a real grown-up present, just as if Aunt Elsie had made it."

"And it isn't half done yet," Ellen answered proudly. "Grandma is helping me with cross-stitch letters in blue and red for one end."

"If I could only make something nice like that! Can't you think of something for me?"

"A hemmed handkerchief?" suggested Ellen.

"Oh, no! Mother has lots of handkerchiefs."

"Yes, but when I gave her one for her birthday she said she had never had enough handkerchiefs. They were like asparagus."

"They don't look like asparagus," Sally replied, loath to criticize her mother but evidently confused. "Anyway, I don't want to give her a handkerchief."

"A penwiper?"

"No, I'm giving Father that."

"A new pincushion cover?"

"Oh! no, Ellen. I'm sick of those presents. I want it to be a big—lovely—Something—a great surprise."

Ellen thought a minute. She was usually resourceful and she did not like to fail her little sister. They had both been earning money all through November and perhaps this was a time to *buy* a present for Mother—even if Grandma disapproved.

"I know that Mother has made out a new list," she said. "She and Father were laughing about it

last night in the library. Let's go and see if it is there."

They found two papers on the desk, unmistakably lists. They were typewritten. Father's was very short: "Anything wrapped up in tissue paper with a red ribbon around it."

"Isn't Father funny?" giggled Ellen. "I'd like to fool him and do up a dead mouse for his stocking."

Mother had filled a full page with her wants. Ellen read out slowly:

Pair of Old English silver peppers
Fur coat
("Father will give her that.")
Umbrella
Robert Frost's Poems
Silk stockings
Muffin tins
Small watering pot for house plants
Handkerchiefs
Guest towels
("Aren't you glad she asked for that?" Sally
    broke in.)
Knitted wash cloths
A red pencil
A blue pencil
Ink eraser
Pen holders
Rubber bands
Hot water bag cover
    A quart of judgment

This last item was scribbled in pencil at the bottom of the sheet.

As Ellen finished reading, she said with what Sally called her "little-mother air," "You needn't worry at all about Mother's present. There are lots of things here you could make for her. Couldn't you do a hot water bag cover if Grandma cut it out for you? I'm sure you could. You take a nice soft piece of old flannel. . . ."

"No! No! Nothing made out of old flannel!" cried Sally. "That's such a baby thing. I want it to be different—and a great surprise. I wish I could

give her the silver peppers.... That's the first thing on her list; but I've only got two dollars and three cents in my bank and I'm afraid that's not enough."

"Oh! It isn't the peppers she wants most!" cried Ellen. "It's the *last* thing she wrote down—that 'quart of judgment.' I know for I heard her tell Father, 'I need that more than anything else...even a pint would help.' And then they both laughed."

"What is judgment?" asked Sally

"It's what the judge gives—a judgment," her sister answered. "It must be something to do with the law."

"Then I know it would cost more than two dollars and three cents," said Sally. "Father said the other day that nothing was so expensive as the law."

"But she only asked for a pint," Ellen objected. "A pint of anything couldn't be very expensive, unless it was diamonds and rubies."

"She wanted a *quart*," Sally corrected. "And she just said that afterwards about a pint helping because she knew a whole quart would be too much for us to buy."

"A hot water bag cover would be lots easier," cautioned Ellen.

"I don't want it to be easy!" cried Sally. "I want it to be what she wants!"

"Well, perhaps you could get it cheap from Uncle John," Ellen suggested. "He's a lawyer—and he's coming to dinner tonight, so you could ask him."

Sally was not afraid to ask Uncle John anything. He never laughed at her or teased her as Uncle Tom sometimes did and he always talked to her as if she were grown up. On any vexed question he always sided with her and Ellen. He had even been known to say before Mother that coconut cake was good for children and that seven-thirty for big girls of seven and eight was a disgracefully early bedtime. He thought arctics unnecessary in winter and when a picnic was planned, he always knew it would be a fine day.

Sally drew him into the little library that evening and shut the door carefully.

"Is it something very important?" he asked as they seated themselves on the sofa.

"Yes," she answered. "Awfully important. It's a secret. You won't tell, will you?"

"No, cross my heart and swear. What is it?"

"It's—it's...Oh—Uncle John—what *is* judgment? I must get some."

"Judgment? That *is* an important question, my dear." Uncle John seemed puzzled for a moment. "And it is hard to answer. Why do you bother about that now? You have your whole life to get it....Come to me again when you're eighteen."

"But I can't wait so long. I must get it right away. Mother wants it for a Christmas present. She put on her list, 'A quart of judgment.' She said even a pint would help."

Uncle John laughed. He threw back his head and shouted. Sally had never seen him laugh so hard. He shook the sofa with his mirth and tears rolled down his cheeks. He didn't stop until he saw that Sally was hurt—and even then a whirlwind of chuckles seized him occasionally.

"I'm not laughing at you, Sally darling," he explained at last, patting her shoulder affectionately, "but at your mother. She doesn't need judgment. She has it. She always has had it. She's a mighty fine woman—your mother. She must have put that on her list as a joke."

"Oh no! Excuse me, Uncle John," Sally protested. "She told Father she wanted it more than anything else. Wouldn't it be a good Christmas present?"

"Perfectly swell," her uncle answered. "The most useful. If you have any left over, give me some."

"Why, I was going to ask you to sell me some," Sally explained. "Ellen said you would surely have it."

Just then Mother called "Ellen! Sally! Bedtime. Hurry, dears. It's twenty minutes to eight already."

"Bother!" exclaimed Sally. "I'm always having

to go to bed. But please tell me where I can get it. At Macy's? Delia is taking us to town tomorrow."

"No, my dear," he answered. "Macy sells almost everything but not that. It doesn't come by the yard."

"Girls!" Mother's voice again.

"Oh! Quick, Uncle John," whispered Sally. "Mother's coming. I'll have to go. Just tell me. What *is* judgment?"

"It is *sense*, Sally," he answered, quite solemn and serious now. "Common sense. But it takes a lot...." He could not finish the sentence for at this point Mother opened the door and carried Sally off to bed.

The little girl snuggled down under the sheets very happily. Uncle John had cleared her mind of all doubt. She had only time for an ecstatic whisper to Ellen before Delia put out the light: "It's all right about Mother's present. Uncle John said it would be 'swell.'" Then she began to calculate: "If it is just cents, common cents, I have ever so many in my bank and I can earn some more. Perhaps I have enough already."

With this delicious hope she fell asleep.

The first thing after breakfast the next morning she opened her bank. It was in the shape of a fat man sitting in a chair. When you put a penny in his hand he nodded his head in gratitude as the money slipped into his safetybox. Sally unscrewed the bottom of this and two dollars and three cents rolled out. It was not all in pennies. There were several nickels, three dimes, two quarters and a fifty-cent piece. It made a rich-looking pile. Sally ran to the kitchen for a pint cup and then up to the nursery to pour her wealth into it. No one was there in the room to hear her cry of disappointment. The coins did not reach to the "Half" marked on the measure.

But there was still hope. The half dollar and quarters when they were changed would lift the level of course. She put all the silver into her pocket and consulted Ellen.

Her sister had passed the penny-bank stage and kept her money in a blue leather purse which was a proud possession. Aunt Elsie had given it to her last Christmas. It had two compartments and a small looking-glass—but there was very little money in it now. Ellen had already bought a good many presents. She was only able to change one quarter and one dime.

"Let's ask Derek," she said. "He loves to open his bank because he can use the screwdriver of his tool set."

Derek was delighted to show his savings—forty-five cents—but he was reluctant to give them all up for one quarter and two dimes. It would mean only three pieces to drop into the chimney of the little red house which was his bank.

"They don't clink at all," he complained, experimenting with the coins Sally held out. "You'll take all my money. I won't have hardly anything."

"You'll have *just* as much money to spend," explained Ellen.

"Yes," Derek admitted, "but not to jingle. I like the jingle. It sounds so much more."

He finally decided to change one nickel and one dime.

Then Grandma changed a dime and Sally had sixty pennies all together to put into the pint cup. They brought the pile up about an inch.

When father came home that night she asked him to change the fifty-cent piece, the quarter and the three nickels, but he did not have ninety cents in pennies and he said that he could not get them until Monday and now it was only Saturday.

"You understand, Sally," he explained looking down into his little daughter's anxious face, "you don't have any more money after this is changed. It only looks more."

"I know, but I want it that way," she answered.

On Monday night he brought her the change

and it made a full inch more of money in the cup. Still it was less than half a pint. Sally confided her discouragement to Ellen.

"Are you sure," asked her sister, "that it was this kind of present Mother wanted? She never asked for money before."

"I'm sure," Sally replied. "Uncle John said it was *cents* and that it would take a lot. Besides she prayed for it in church yesterday—so she must want it awfully."

"Prayed for it!" exclaimed Ellen in surprise.

"Yes. I heard her. It's that prayer we all say together. She asked God for 'two cents of all thy mercies.'"

"But if she wants a whole pint why did she only ask for 'two cents'?" demanded the practical Ellen.

"I don't know," Sally answered. "Perhaps she thought it would be greedy. Mother is never greedy."

For several days things were at a standstill. Ellen caught a cold and passed it on to Sally and Derek. They were all put to bed and could do very little Christmas work. While Mother read aloud to them Sally finished her penwiper for Father and decorated a blotter for Uncle John—but sewing on Grandma's pincushion cover was difficult because the pillow at Sally's back kept slipping and she couldn't keep the needle straight. There seemed no way of adding anything to the pint cup.

"Mother, how could I earn some money quickly before Christmas?" Sally asked the first day that she was up.

"You have already earned a good deal, dear," Mother said. "Do you really need more?"

"Yes, Mother, lots more."

"How about getting 100 in your number work? Father gives you a dime every time you do that."

"Yes," sighed Sally, "but it's very hard to get all the examples right. Don't you think when I get all right but one he might give me nine cents?"

"No," said Mother laughing. "Your father be-

lieves that nothing is good in arithmetic but 100."

She did earn one dime that way and then school closed, leaving no hope for anything more before Christmas.

On the twentieth of December there was a windfall. Aunt Elsie, who usually spent the holidays with them, was in the South and she sent Mother four dollars—one for each child for a Christmas present. "She told me to buy something for you," Mother explained, "but I thought perhaps you might like to spend the money yourselves—later on—during vacation."

"Oh! I'd like my dollar right away!" cried Sally delightedly. "And," she added rather shamefacedly, "Lovey is so little... do you think she needs all her money? Couldn't she give me half hers?"

"Why Sally, I'm surprised at you!" her mother answered. "I can't take your little sister's share for you. It wouldn't be fair. I am buying a new *Benjamin Bunny* for Lovey."

Aunt Elsie's gift brought the pennies in the pint cup a little above the half mark.

On the twenty-first Sally earned five cents by sweeping off the back porch. This had been a regular source of revenue in the fall, but when the dead leaves gave place to snow Mother forbade the sweeping. On the twenty-first there was no snow and Sally was allowed to go out with her little broom.

On the twenty-second Ellen and Sally went to a birthday party and Sally found a shiny bright dime in her piece of birthday cake. This helped a little. She and Ellen spent all their spare moments in shaking up the pennies in the pint measure—but they could not bring the level much above "One Half." Ellen was as excited over the plan now as Sally and she generously added her last four cents to the pile.

On the twenty-third Sally made a final desperate effort. "Mother," she said, "Uncle John is coming to dinner again tonight. Do you think he

would be willing to give me my birthday dollar now?"

Mother smiled as she answered slowly—"But your birthday isn't till June. Isn't it rather strange to ask for your present so long ahead? Where is all this money going to?"

"It's a secret! My special secret!" cried the little girl, taking her mother's reply for consent.

Uncle John gave her the dollar. She hugged and kissed him with delight and he said, "Let me always be your banker, Sally. I'm sorry you are so hard up, but don't take any wooden nickels."

"'Wooden nickels,'" she repeated slowly.

"What are they? Perhaps they would fill up the bottom—"

"Of your purse?" Uncle John finished the sentence for her. "No, no, my dear. They are a very poor bottom for anything—and they are worse on top."

"It wasn't my purse," said Sally. "It was—but it's a secret."

When Father changed the birthday dollar into pennies he said, "You are getting to be a regular little miser, my dear. I don't understand it. Where is all this money going to?"

"That's just what Mother asked," Sally

answered. "It's a secret. You'll know on Christmas. Oh, Father, I think I have enough now!"

But she hadn't. The pennies seemed to melt away as they fell into the measure. She and Ellen took them all out three times and put them back again shaking them sideways and forwards, but it was no use. They looked a mountain on the nursery floor but they shrank in size the moment they were put inside that big cup. The mark stood obstinately below "Three Quarters."

"Oh! Ellen!" sobbed Sally after the third attempt. "Not even a pint! It's a horrid mean little present! All my presents are horrid. I never can give nice things like you! Oh dear, what shall I do!"

"Don't cry, Sally—please don't," said Ellen trying to comfort her little sister. "It's not a horrid present. It will look lovely when you put tissue paper around it and lots of red ribbon and a card. It *sounds* so much more than it looks," Ellen went on, giving the cup a vigorous jerk. "Why don't you print on your card 'Shake well before opening,' like our cough mixture?"

"I might," assented Sally, only partly reassured.

She had believed up to the last moment that she would be able to carry out her plan. It was vaguely associated in her mind with a miracle. Anything might happen at Christmas time but this year she had hoped for too much. It was so late now however that there was nothing to do but make the outside of her gift look as attractive as possible. She and Ellen spent most of the afternoon before Christmas wrapping up their presents. The pint cup was a little awkward in shape but they had it well covered and the red satin ribbon gathered tight at the top before Grandma made the final bow. It was a real rosette, for Sally had asked for something special.

Christmas Eve was almost more fun than Christmas. The Tuckers made a ceremony of hanging up their stockings. The whole family formed a line in the upper hall with Father at the head, the youngest child on his back, and then they marched downstairs keeping step to a Christmas chant. It was a home-made nonsense verse with a chorus of "Doodley-doodley, doodley-doo!" which everybody shouted. By the time they reached the living-room the line was in wild spirits.

The stockings were always hung in the same places. Father had the big armchair to the right of the fireplace and Mother the large mahogany chair opposite it, Lovey had a small white chair borrowed from the nursery. Derek tied his sock to the hook which usually held the fire tongs above the wood basket (it was a very inconvenient place but he liked it) and Ellen and Sally divided the sofa.

After the stockings were put up, one of the children recited the Bible verses, "And there were in the same country shepherds abiding in the field, keeping watch over their flock by night," through "Mary kept all these things and pondered them in her heart." Sally had said the verses last Christmas—Ellen the year before—and now it was Derek's turn. He only forgot once and Ellen prompted him softly.

Then they all sang Holy Night—and Father read "'Twas the Night Before Christmas." Last of all, the children distributed their gifts for the family—with a great many stern directions: "Mother, you won't look at this till tomorrow, will you? Father, you promise not to peek?" Then they went up to bed and by morning Father and Mother and Santa Claus had the stockings stuffed full of things.

It went off as usual this year but through all the singing and the shouting Sally had twinges of disappointment thinking of Mother's unfinished present. She had squeezed it into Mother's stocking with some difficulty. Then came Ellen's lovely towel and on top of that Derek's calendar which he had made in school.

There was a family rule at the Tuckers' that stockings were not opened until after breakfast.

Mother said that presents on an empty stomach were bad for temper and digestion and though it was hard to swallow your cereal Christmas morning, the children knew it was no use protesting.

The first sight of the living-room was wonderful. The place had completely changed over night. Of course the stockings were knobby with unknown delights, and there were packages everywhere, on the tables and chairs, and on the floor big express boxes that had come from distant places, marked "Do Not Open Until Christmas."

Some presents are of such unmistakable shape that they cannot be hidden. Last year Derek had jumped right onto his rocking horse shouting, "It's mine! I know it's mine!" This morning he caught sight of a drum and looked no further. Lovey fell upon a white plush bunny. A lovely pink parasol was sticking out of the top of Sally's stocking and Ellen had a blue one. They just unfurled them over their heads and then watched Father and Mother unwrapping their presents.

The girls felt Derek and Lovey were very young because they emptied their stockings without a look towards the two big armchairs. That was the most thrilling moment, when your own offering came to view and Mother said, "Just what I wanted!" or Father, "How did you know I needed a penwiper?"

Mother always opened the children's presents first. She was untying the red ribbon on Ellen's towel now and reading the card which said "Every stitch a stitch of love." As she pulled off the tissue paper she exclaimed, "What beautiful work! What exquisite little stitches! Ellen—I am proud of you. This is a charming guest towel. Thank you, dear, so much."

"Grandma marked the cross-stitch for me," explained Ellen, "but I did all the rest myself."

Sally shivered with excitement as Mother's hand went down into her stocking again and tugged at the tin cup.

"Here is something very heavy," she said. "I can't guess what it is, and the card says 'Merry Christmas to Mother from Sally. Shake well before opening.' Is it medicine or cologne?"

Nobody remembered just what happened after that. Perhaps Grandma's bow was not tied tightly enough, perhaps Mother tilted the cup as she shook it, but in a moment all the pennies were on the floor. They rolled everywhere, past the chairs, into the grate, under the sofa and on to the remotest corners of the room. There was a terrific scramble. Father and Mother and Ellen and Sally and Derek, even Grandma and Lovey got down on their hands and knees to pick them up. They bumped elbows and knocked heads together and this onrush sent the coins flying everywhere. The harder they were chased the more perversely they hid themselves. Out of the hubbub Mother cried, "Sally dear, what is this? I don't understand. All your Christmas money for me? Darling, I can't take it."

Sally flung herself into her mother's arms with a sob. "Oh! you must!" she begged. "I'm sorry it's not a whole pint. I tried so hard. You said—you said—you wanted it most of all."

"Most of all?"

"Yes, judgment, cents. Uncle John said it was cents. You said even a pint would help. Won't half a pint be some good?"

Father and Mother and Grandma all laughed then. Father laughed almost as hard as Uncle John did when he first heard of Mother's list, and he declared that he was going to take Sally into the bank as a partner. But Mother lifted the little girl into her lap and whispered, "It's the most wonderful present I ever had. There's nothing so wonderful as sense—except love."

A Miserable, Merry Christmas

LINCOLN STEFFENS

My father's business seems to have been one of slow but steady growth. He and his local partner, Llewelen Tozer, had no vices. They were devoted to their families and to "the store," which grew with the town, which, in turn, grew and changed with the State from a gambling, mining, and ranching community to one of farming, fruit-raising, and building. Immigration poured in, not gold-seekers now, but farmers, businessmen and home-builders, who settled, planted, reaped, and traded in the natural riches of the State, which prospered greatly, "making" the people who will tell you that they "made the State."

As the store made money and I was getting through the primary school, my father bought a lot uptown, at Sixteenth and K Streets, and built us a "big" house. It was off the line of the city's growth, but it was near a new grammar school for me and my sisters, who were coming along fast after me. This interested the family, not me. They were always talking about school; they had not had much of it themselves, and they thought they had missed something. My father used to write speeches, my mother verses, and their theory seems to have been that they had talents which a school would have brought to flower. They agreed, therefore, that their children's gifts should have all the schooling there was. My view, then, was that I had had a good deal of it already, and I was not interested at all. It interfered with my own business, with my own education.

And indeed I remember very little of the primary school. I learned to read, write, spell, and count, and reading was all right. I had a practi-cal use for books, which I searched for ideas and parts to play with, characters to be, lives to live. The primary school was probably a good one, but I cannot remember learning anything except to read aloud "perfectly" from a teacher whom I adored and who was fond of me. She used to embrace me before the whole class and she favored me openly to the scandal of the other pupils, who called me "teacher's pet." Their scorn did not trouble me; I saw and I said that they envied me. I paid for her favor, however. When she married I had queer, unhappy feelings of resentment; I didn't want to meet her husband, and when I had to I wouldn't speak to him. He laughed, and she kissed me—happily for her, to me offensively. I never would see her again. Through with her, I fell in love immediately with Miss Kay, another grown young woman who wore glasses and had a fine, clear skin. I did not know her, I only saw her in the street, but once I followed her, found out where she lived, and used to pass her house, hoping to see her, and yet choking with embarrassment if I did. This fascination lasted for years; it was still a sort of super-romance to me when later I was "going with" another girl nearer my own age.

What interested me in our new neighborhood was not the school, nor the room I was to have in the house all to myself, but the stable which was built back of the house. My father let me direct the making of a stall, a little smaller than the other stalls, for my pony, and I prayed and hoped and my sister Lou believed that that meant that I would get the pony, perhaps for Christmas. I pointed out to her that there were three other stalls and no horses at all. This I said

in order that she should answer it. She could not. My father, sounded, said that some day we might have horses and a cow; meanwhile a stable added to the value of a house. "Some day" is a pain to a boy who lives in and knows only "now." My good little sisters, to comfort me, remarked that Christmas was coming, but Christmas was always coming and grown-ups were always talking about it, asking you what you wanted and then giving you what they wanted you to have. Though everybody knew what I wanted, I told them all again. My mother knew that I told God, too, every night. I wanted a pony, and to make sure that they understood, I declared that I wanted nothing else.

"Nothing but a pony?" my father asked.

"Nothing," I said.

"Not even a pair of high boots?"

That was hard. I did want boots, but I stuck to the pony. "No, not even boots."

"Nor candy? There ought to be something to fill your stocking with, and Santa Claus can't put a pony into a stocking."

That was true, and he couldn't lead a pony down the chimney either. But no. "All I want is a pony," I said. "If I can't have a pony, give me nothing, nothing."

Now I had been looking myself for the pony I wanted, going to sales stables, inquiring of horsemen, and I had seen several that would do. My father let me "try" them. I tried so many ponies that I was learning fast to sit a horse. I chose several, but my father always found some fault with them. I was in despair. When Christmas was at hand I had given up all hope of a pony, and on Christmas Eve I hung up my stocking along with my sisters', of whom, by the way, I now had three. I haven't mentioned them or their coming because, you understand, they were girls, and girls, young girls, counted for nothing in my manly life. They did not mind me either; they were so happy that Christmas Eve that I caught some of their merriment. I speculated on what I'd get; I hung up the biggest

stocking I had, and we all went reluctantly to bed to wait till morning. Not to sleep; not right away. We were told that we must not only sleep promptly, we must not wake up till seven-thirty the next morning—or if we did, we must not go to the fireplace for our Christmas. Impossible.

We did sleep that night, but we woke up at six A.M. We lay in our beds and debated through the open doors whether to obey till, say, half-past six. Then we bolted. I don't know who started it, but there was a rush. We all disobeyed; we raced to disobey and get first to the fireplace in the front room downstairs. And there they were, the gifts, all sorts of wonderful things, mixed-up piles of presents; only, as I disentangled the mess, I saw that my stocking was empty; it hung limp; not a thing in it; and under an around it—nothing. My sisters had knelt down, each by her pile of gifts; they were squealing with delight, till they looked up and saw me standing there in my nightgown with nothing. They left their piles to come to me and look with me at my empty place. Nothing. They felt my stocking: nothing.

I don't remember whether I cried at that moment, but my sisters did. They ran with me back to my bed, and there we all cried till I became indignant. That helped some. I got up, dressed, and driving my sisters away, I went alone out into the yard, down to the stable, and there, all by myself, I wept. My mother came out to me by and by; she found me in my pony stall, sobbing on the floor, and she tried to comfort me. But I heard my father outside; he had come part way with her, and she was having some sort of angry quarrel with him. She tried to comfort me; besought me to come to breakfast. I could not; I wanted no comfort and no breakfast. She left me and went on into the house with sharp words for my father.

I don't know what kind of a breakfast the family had. My sisters said it was "awful." They were ashamed to enjoy their own toys. They came to me, and I was rude. I ran away from

them. I went around to the front of the house, sat down on the steps, and, the crying over, I ached. I was wronged, I was hurt—I can feel now what I felt then, and I am sure that if one could see the wounds upon our hearts, there would be found still upon mine a scar from that terrible Christmas morning. And my father, the practical joker, he must have been hurt, too, a little. I saw him looking out of the window. He was watching me or something for an hour or two, drawing back the curtain ever so little lest I catch him, but I saw his face, and I think I can see now the anxiety upon it, the worried impatience.

After—I don't know how long—surely an hour or two—I was brought to the climax of my agony by the sight of a man riding a pony down the street, a pony and a brand-new saddle; the most beautiful saddle I ever saw, and it was a boy's saddle; the man's feet were not in the stirrups; his legs were too long. The outfit was perfect; it was the realization of all my dreams, the answer to all my prayers. A fine new bridle, with a light curb bit. And the pony! As he drew near,

I saw that the pony was really a small horse, what we called an Indian pony, a bay, with black mane and tail, and one white foot and a white star on his forehead. For such a horse as that I would have given, I could have forgiven, anything.

But the man, a disheveled fellow with a blackened eye and a fresh-cut face, came along, reading the numbers on the houses, and, as my hopes—my impossible hopes—rose, he looked at our door and passed by, he and the pony, and the saddle and the bridle. Too much. I fell upon the steps, and having wept before, I broke now into such a flood of tears that I was a floating wreck when I heard a voice.

"Say, kid," it said, "do you know a boy named Lennie Steffens?"

I looked up. It was the man on the pony, back again, at our horse block.

"Yes," I spluttered through my tears. "That's me."

"Well," he said, "then this is your horse. I've been looking all over for you and your house. Why don't you put your number where it can be seen?"

"Get down," I said, running out to him.

He went on saying something about "ought to have got here at seven o'clock; told me to bring the nag here and tie him to your post and leave him for you. But, hell, I got into a drunk—and a fight—and a hospital, and—"

"Get down," I said.

He got down, and he boosted me up to the saddle. He offered to fit the stirrups to me, but I didn't want him to. I wanted to ride.

"What's the matter with you?" he said, angrily. "What you crying for? Don't you like the horse? He's a dandy, this horse. I know him of old. He's fine at cattle; he'll drive 'em alone."

I hardly heard, I could scarcely wait, but he persisted. He adjusted the stirrups, and then, finally, off I rode, slowly, at a walk, so happy, so thrilled, that I did not know what I was doing. I did not look back at the house or the man, I rode off up the street, taking note of everything—of the reins, of the pony's long mane, of the carved leather saddle. I had never seen anything so beautiful. And mine! I was going to ride up past Miss Kay's house. But I noticed on the horn of the saddle some stains like rain-drops, so I turned and trotted home, not to the house but to the stable. There was the family, father, mother, sisters, all working for me, all happy. They had been putting in place the tools of my new business: blankets, curry-comb, brush, pitchfork—everything, and there was hay in the loft.

"What did you come back so soon for?" somebody asked. "Why didn't you go on riding?"

I pointed to the stains. "I wasn't going to get my new saddle rained on," I said. And my father laughed. "It isn't raining," he said. "Those are not rain-drops."

"They are tears," my mother gasped, and she gave my father a look which sent him off to the house. Worse still, my mother offered to wipe away the tears still running out of my eyes. I gave her such a look as she had given him, and she went off after my father, drying her own tears. My sisters remained and we all unsaddled the pony, put on his halter, led him to his stall, tied and fed him. It began really to rain; so all the rest of that memorable day we curried and combed that pony. The girls plaited his mane, forelock, and tail, while I pitchforked hay to him and curried and brushed, curried and brushed. For a change we brought him out to drink; we led him up and down, blanketed like a race-horse; we took turns at that. But the best, the most inexhaustible fun, was to clean him. When we went reluctantly to our midday Christmas dinner, we all smelt of horse, and my sisters had to wash their faces and hands. I was asked to, but I wouldn't, till my mother bade me look in the mirror. Then I washed up—quick. My face was caked with the muddy lines of tears that had coursed over my cheeks to my mouth. Having washed away that shame, I ate my dinner, and as I ate I grew hungrier and hungrier. It was my first meal that day, and as I filled up on the turkey and the stuffing, the cranberries and the pies, the fruit and the nuts—as I swelled, I could laugh. My mother said I still choked and sobbed now and then, but I laughed, too; I saw and enjoyed my sisters' presents till—I had to go out and attend to my pony, who was there, really and truly there, the promise, the beginning, of a happy double life. And—I went and looked to make sure—there was the saddle, too, and the bridle.

But that Christmas, which my father had planned so carefully, was it the best or the worst I ever knew? He often asked me that; I never could answer as a boy. I think now that it was both. It covered the whole distance from broken-hearted misery to bursting happiness—too fast. A grown-up could hardly have stood it.

The Miraculous Staircase

ARTHUR GORDON

On that cool December morning in 1878, sunlight lay like an amber rug across the dusty streets and adobe houses of Santa Fe. It glinted on the bright tile roof of the almost completed Chapel of Our Lady of Light and on the nearby windows of the convent school run by the Sisters of Loretto. Inside the convent, the Mother Superior looked up from her packing as a tap came on her door.

"It's *another* carpenter, Reverend Mother," said Sister Francis Louise, her round face apologetic. "I told him that you're leaving right away, that you haven't time to see him, but he says. . . ."

"I know what he says," Mother Magdalene said, going on resolutely with her packing. "That he's heard about our problem with the new chapel. That he's the best carpenter in all of New Mexico. That he can build us a staircase to the choir loft despite the fact that the brilliant architect in Paris who drew the plans failed to leave any space for one. And despite the fact that five master carpenters have already tried and failed. You're quite right, Sister; I don't have time to listen to that story again."

"But he seems such a nice man," said Sister Francis Louise wistfully, "and he's out there with his burro, and. . . ."

"I'm sure," said Mother Magdalene with a smile, "that he's a charming man, and that his burro is a charming donkey. But there's sickness down at the Santo Domingo pueblo, and it may be cholera. Sister Mary Helen and I are the only ones here who've had cholera. So we have to go. And you have to stay and run the school. And that's that!" Then she called, "Manuela!"

A young Indian girl of 12 or 13, black-haired and smiling, came in quietly on moccasined feet. She was a mute. She could hear and understand, but the Sisters had been unable to teach her to speak. The Mother Superior spoke to her gently: "Take my things down to the wagon, child. I'll be right there." And to Sister Francis Louise: "You'd better tell your carpenter friend to come back in two or three weeks. I'll see him then."

"Two or three weeks! Surely you'll be home for Christmas?"

"If it's the Lord's will, Sister. I hope so."

In the street, beyond the waiting wagon, Mother Magdalene could see the carpenter, a bearded man, strongly built and taller than most Mexicans, with dark eyes and a smiling, windburned face. Beside him, laden with tools and scraps of lumber, a small gray burro stood patiently. Manuela was stroking its nose, glancing shyly at its owner. "You'd better explain," said the Mother Superior, "that the child can hear him, but she can't speak."

Goodbyes were quick—the best kind when you leave a place you love. Southwest, then, along the dusty trail, the mountains purple with shadow, the Rio Grande a ribbon of green far off to the right. The pace was slow, but Mother Magdalene and Sister Mary Helen amused themselves by singing songs and telling Christmas stories as the sun marched up and down the sky. And their leathery driver listened and nodded.

Two days of this brought them to Santo Domingo Pueblo, where the sickness was not cholera after all, but measles, almost as deadly in an Indian village. And so they stayed, helping

the harassed Father Sebastian, visiting the dark adobe hovels where feverish brown children tossed and fierce Indian dogs showed their teeth.

At night they were bone-weary, but sometimes Mother Magdalene found time to talk to Father Sebastian about her plans for the dedication of the new chapel. It was to be in April; the Archbishop himself would be there. And it might have been dedicated sooner, were it not for this incredible business of a choir loft with no means of access—unless it were a ladder.

"I told the Bishop," said Mother Magdalene, "that it would be a mistake to have the plans drawn in Paris. If something went wrong, what could we do? But he wanted our chapel in Santa Fe patterned after the Sainte Chapelle in Paris, and who am I to argue with Bishop Lamy? So the talented Monsieur Mouly designs a beautiful choir loft high up under the rose window, and no way to get to it."

"Perhaps," sighed Father Sebastian, "he had in mind a heavenly choir. The kind with wings."

"It's not funny," said Mother Magdalene a bit sharply. "I've prayed and prayed, but apparently there's no solution at all. There just isn't room on the chapel floor for the supports such a staircase needs."

The days passed, and with each passing day Christmas drew closer. Twice, horsemen on their way from Santa Fe to Albuquerque brought letters from Sister Francis Louise. All was well at the convent, but Mother Magdalene frowned over certain paragraphs. "The children are getting ready for Christmas," Sister Francis Louise wrote in her first letter. "Our little Manuela and the carpenter have become great friends. It's amazing how much he seems to know about us all...."

And what, thought Mother Magdalene, is the carpenter still doing there?

The second letter also mentioned the carpenter. "Early every morning he comes with another load of lumber, and every night he goes away. When we ask him by what authority he does these things, he smiles and says nothing. We have tried to pay him for his work, but he will accept no pay...."

Work? What work? Mother Magdalene wrinkled up her nose in exasperation. Had that softhearted Sister Francis Louise given the man permission to putter around in the new chapel? With firm and disapproving hand, the Mother Superior wrote a note ordering an end to all such unauthorized activities. She gave it to an Indian pottery-maker on his way to Santa Fe.

But that night the first snow fell, so thick and heavy that the Indian turned back. Next day at noon the sun shone again on a world glittering with diamonds. But Mother Magdalene knew that another snowfall might make it impossible for her to be home for Christmas. By now the sickness at Santo Domingo was subsiding. And so that afternoon they began the long ride back.

The snow did come again, making their slow progress even slower. It was late on Christmas Eve, close to midnight, when the tired horses plodded up to the convent door. But lamps still burned. Manuela flew down the steps, Sister Francis Louise close behind her. And chilled and weary though she was, Mother Magdalene sensed instantly an excitement, an electricity in the air that she could not understand.

Nor did she understand it when they led her, still in her heavy wraps, down the corridor, into the new, as-yet-unusedchapel where a few candles burned. "Look, Reverend Mother," breathed Sister Francis Louise. "Look!"

Like a curl of smoke the staircase rose before them, as insubstantial as a dream. Its top rested against the choir loft. Nothing else supported it; it seemed to float on air. There were no banisters. Two complete spirals it made, the polished wood gleaming softly in the candlelight. "Thirty-three steps," whispered Sister Francis Louise. "One for each year in the life of Our Lord."

Mother Magdalene moved forward like a woman in a trance. She put her foot on the first step, then the second, then the third. There was not a tremor. She looked down, bewildered, at Manuela's ecstatic, upturned face. "But it's impossible! There wasn't time!"

"He finished yesterday," the Sister said. "He didn't come today. No one has seen him anywhere in Santa Fe. He's gone."

"But *who* was he? Don't you even know his *name?*"

The Sister shook her head, but now Manuela pushed forward, nodding emphatically. Her mouth opened; she took a deep, shuddering breath; she made a sound that was like a gasp in the stillness. The nuns stared at her, transfixed. She tried again. This time it was a syllable, followed by another. "Jo-sé." She clutched the Mother Superior's arm and repeated the first word she had ever spoken. "José!"

Sister Francis Louise crossed herself. Mother Magdalene felt her heart contract. José—the Spanish word for Joseph. Joseph the Carpenter. Joseph the Master Woodworker of. . . .

"José!" Manuela's dark eyes were full of tears. "José!"

Silence, then, in the shadowy chapel. No one moved. Far away across the snow-silvered town Mother Magdalene heard a bell tolling midnight. She came down the stairs and took Manuela's hand. She felt uplifted by a great surge of wonder and gratitude and compassion and love. And she knew what it was. It was the spirit of Christmas. And it was upon them all.

Author's Note. You may see the inexplicable staircase itself in Santa Fe today. It stands just as it stood when the chapel was dedicated almost a hundred years ago—except for the banister, which was added later. Tourists stare and marvel. Architects shake their heads and murmur, "Impossible." No one knows the identity of the designer-builder. All the Sisters know is that the problem existed, a stranger came, solved it and left.

The 33 steps make two complete turns without central support. There are no nails in the staircase; only wooden pegs. The curved stringers are put together with exquisite precision; the wood is spliced in seven places on the inside and nine on the outside. The wood is said to be a hard-fir variety, nonexistent in New Mexico. School records show that no payment for the staircase was ever made.

Our Lady's Juggler

ANATOLE FRANCE

In the days of King Louis there was a poor juggler in France, a native of Compiègne, Barnaby by name, who went about from town to town performing feats of skill and strength.

On fair days he would unfold an old worn-out carpet in the public square, and when by means of a jovial address, which he had learned of a very ancient juggler, and which he never varied in the least, he had drawn together the children and loafers, he assumed extraordinary attitudes, and balanced a tin plate on the tip of his nose. At first the crowd would feign indifference.

But when, supporting himself on his hands face downwards, he threw into the air six copper balls, which glittered in the sunshine, and caught them again with his feet; or when throwing himself backwards until his heels and the nape of the neck met, giving his body the form of a perfect wheel, he would juggle in this posture with a dozen knives, a murmur of admiration would escape the spectators, and pieces of money rain down upon the carpet.

Nevertheless, like the majority of those who live by their wits, Barnaby of Compiègne had a great struggle to make a living.

Earning his bread in the sweat of his brow, he bore rather more than his share of the penalties consequent upon the misdoings of our father Adam.

Again, he was unable to work as constantly as he would have been willing to do. The warmth of the sun and the broad daylight were as necessary to enable him to display his brilliant parts as to the trees if flower and fruit should be expected of them. In winter time he was nothing more than a tree stripped of its leaves, and as it were dead. The frozen ground was hard to the juggler, and, like the grasshopper of which Marie de France tells us, the inclement season caused him to suffer both cold and hunger. But as he was simple-natured he bore his ills patiently.

He had never meditated on the origin of wealth, nor upon the inequality of human conditions. He believed firmly that if this life should prove hard, the life to come could not fail to redress the balance, and this hope upheld him. He did not resemble those thievish and miscreant Merry Andrews who sell their souls to the devil. He never blasphemed God's name; he lived uprightly, and although he had no wife of his own, he did not covet his neighbour's, since woman is ever the enemy of the strong man, as it appears by the history of Samson recorded in the Scriptures.

In truth, his was not a nature much disposed to carnal delights, and it was a greater deprivation to him to forsake the tankard than the Hebe who bore it. For whilst not wanting in sobriety, he was fond of a drink when the weather waxed hot. He was a worthy man who feared God, and was very devoted to the Blessed Virgin.

Never did he fail on entering a church to fall upon his knees before the image of the Mother of God, and offer up this prayer to her:

"Blessed Lady, keep watch over my life until it shall please God that I die, and when I am dead, ensure to me the possession of the joys of paradise."

Now on a certain evening after a dreary wet day, as Barnaby pursued his road, sad and bent, carrying under his arm his balls and knives wrapped up in his old carpet, on the watch for some barn where, though he might not sup, he might sleep, he perceived on the road, going in the same direction as himself, a monk, whom he saluted courteously. And as they walked at the same rate they fell into conversation with one another.

"Fellow traveller," said the monk, "how comes it about that you are clothed all in green? Is it perhaps in order to take the part of a jester in some mystery play?"

"Not at all, good father," replied Barnaby. "Such as you see me, I am called Barnaby, and for my calling I am a juggler. There would be no pleasanter calling in the world if it would always provide one with daily bread."

"Friend Barnaby," returned the monk, "be careful what you say. There is no calling more pleasant than the monastic life. Those who lead it are occupied with the praises of God, the Blessed Virgin, and the saints; and, indeed, the religious life is one ceaseless hymn to the Lord."

Barnaby replied—

"Good father, I own that I spoke like an ignorant man. Your calling cannot be in any respect compared to mine, and although there may be some merit in dancing with a penny balanced on a stick on the tip of one's nose, it is not a merit which comes within hail of your own. Gladly would I, like you, good father, sing my office day by day, and especially, the office of the most Holy Virgin, to whom I have vowed a singular devotion. In order to embrace the monastic life I would willingly abandon the art by which from Soissons to Beauvais I am well known in upwards of six hundred towns and villages."

The monk was touched by the juggler's simplicity, and as he was not lacking in discernment, he at once recognized in Barnaby one of those men of whom it is said in the Scriptures: Peace on earth to men of good will. And for this reason he replied—

"Friend Barnaby, come with me, and I will have you admitted into the monastery of which I am Prior. He who guided St. Mary of Egypt in the desert set me upon your path to lead you into the way of salvation."

It was in this manner, then, that Barnaby became a monk. In the monastery into which he was received the religious vied with one another in the worship of the Blessed Virgin, and in her honour each employed all the knowledge and all the skill which God had given him.

The prior on his part wrote books dealing according to the rules of scholarship with the virtues of the Mother of God.

Brother Maurice, with a deft hand copied out these treatises upon sheets of vellum.

Brother Alexander adorned the leaves with delicate miniature paintings. Here were displayed the Queen of Heaven seated upon Solomon's throne, and while four lions were on guard at her feet, around the nimbus which encircled her head hovered seven doves, which are the seven gifts of the Holy Spirit, the gifts, namely, of Fear, Piety, Knowledge, Strength, Counsel, Understanding, and Wisdom. For her companions she had six virgins with hair of gold, namely, Humility, Prudence, Seclusion, Submission, Virginity, and Obedience.

At her feet were two little naked figures, perfectly white, in an attitude of supplication. These were souls imploring her all-powerful intercession for their soul's health, and we may be sure not imploring in vain.

Upon another page facing this, Brother Alexander represented Eve, so that the Fall and the Redemption could be perceived at one and the same time—Eve the Wife abased, and Mary the Virgin exalted.

Furthermore, to the marvel of the beholder, this book contained presentments of the Well of Living Waters, the Fountain, the Lily, the

Moon, the Sun, and the Gardens enclosed of which the Song of Songs tells us, the Gate of Heaven and the City of God, and all these things were symbols of the Blessed Virgin.

Brother Marbode was likewise one of the most loving children of Mary.

He spent all his days carving images in stone, so that his beard, his eyebrows, and his hair were white with dust, and his eyes continually swollen and weeping; but his strength and cheerfulness were not diminished, although he was now well gone in years, and it was clear that the Queen of Paradise still cherished her servant in his old age. Marbode represented her seated upon a throne, her brow encircled with an orb-shaped nimbus set with pearls. And he took care that the folds of her dress should cover the feet of her, concerning whom the prophet declared: My beloved is as a garden enclosed.

Sometimes, too, he depicted her in the semblance of a child full of grace, and appearing to say, "Thou art my God, even from my mother's womb."

In the priory, moreover, were poets who composed hymns in Latin, both in prose and verse, in honour of the Blessed Virgin Mary, and amongst the company was even a brother from Picardy who sang the miracles of Our Lady in rhymed verse and in the vulgar tongue.

Being a witness of this emulation in praise and the glorious harvest of their labours, Barnaby mourned his own ignorance and simplicity.

"Alas!" he sighed, as he took his solitary walk in the little shelterless garden of the monastery,

"wretched wight that I am, to be unable, like my brothers, worthily to praise the Holy Mother of God, to whom I have vowed my whole heart's affection. Alas! alas! I am but a rough man and unskilled in the arts, and I can render you in service, blessed Lady, neither edifying sermons, nor treatises set out in order according to rule, nor ingenious paintings, nor statues truthfully sculptured, nor verses whose march is measured to the beat of feet. No gift have I, alas!"

After this fashion he groaned and gave himself up to sorrow. But one evening, when the monks were spending their hour of liberty in conversation, he heard one of them tell the tale of a religious man who could repeat nothing other than the Ave Maria. This poor man was despised for his ignorance; but after his death there issued forth from his mouth five roses in honour of the five letters of the name Mary (Marie), and thus his sanctity was made manifest.

Whilst he listened to this narrative Barnaby marvelled yet once again at the loving kindness of the Virgin; but the lesson of that blessed death did not avail to console him, for his heart overflowed with zeal, and he longed to advance the glory of his Lady, who is in heaven.

How to compass this he sought but could find no way, and day by day he became the more cast down, when one morning he awakened filled full with joy, hastened to the chapel, and remained there alone for more than an hour. After dinner he returned to the chapel once more.

And, starting from that moment, he repaired daily to the chapel at such hours as it was deserted, and spent within it a good part of the time which the other monks devoted to the liberal and mechanical arts. His sadness vanished, nor did he any longer groan.

A demeanour so strange awakened the curiosity of the monks.

These began to ask one another for what purpose Brother Barnaby could be indulging so persistently in retreat.

The prior, whose duty it is to let nothing escape him in the behaviour of his children in religion, resolved to keep a watch over Barnaby during his withdrawals to the chapel. One day, then, when he was shut up there after his custom, the prior, accompanied by two of the older monks, went to discover through the chinks in the door what was going on within the chapel.

They saw Barnaby before the altar of the Blessed Virgin, head downwards, with his feet in the air, and he was juggling with six balls of copper and a dozen knives. In honour of the Holy Mother of God he was performing those feats, which aforetime had won him most renown. Not recognizing that the simple fellow was thus placing at the service of the Blessed Virgin his knowledge and skill, the two old monks exclaimed against the sacrilege.

The prior was aware how stainless was Barnaby's soul, but he concluded that he had been seized with madness. They were all three preparing to lead him swiftly from the chapel, when they saw the Blessed Virgin descend the steps of the altar and advance to wipe away with a fold of her azure robe the sweat which was dropping from her juggler's forehead.

Then the prior, falling upon his face upon the pavement, uttered these words—

"Blessed are the simple-hearted, for they shall see God."

"Amen!" responded the old brethren, and kissed the ground.

Mr. Edwards Meets Santa Claus

LAURA INGALLS WILDER

The days were short and cold, the wind whistled sharply, but there was no snow. Cold rains were falling. Day after day the rain fell, pattering on the roof and pouring from the eaves.

Mary and Laura stayed close by the fire, sewing their nine-patch quilt blocks, or cutting paper dolls from scraps of wrapping-paper, and hearing the wet sound of the rain. Every night was so cold that they expected to see snow next morning, but in the morning they saw only sad, wet grass.

They pressed their noses against the squares of glass in the windows that Pa had made, and they were glad they could see out. But they wished they could see snow.

Laura was anxious because Christmas was near, and Santa Claus and his reindeer could not travel without snow. Mary was afraid that, even if it snowed, Santa Claus could not find them, so far away in Indian Territory. When they asked Ma about this, she said she didn't know.

"What day is it?" they asked her, anxiously. "How many more days till Christmas?" And they counted off the days on their fingers, till there was only one more day left.

Rain was still falling that morning. There was not one crack in the gray sky. They felt almost sure there would be no Christmas. Still, they kept hoping.

Just before noon the light changed. The clouds broke and drifted apart, shining white in a clear blue sky. The sun shone, birds sang, and thousands of drops of water sparkled on the grasses. But when Ma opened the door to let in the fresh, cold air, they heard the creek roaring.

They had not thought about the creek. Now they knew they would have no Christmas, because Santa Claus could not cross that roaring creek.

Pa came in, bringing a big fat turkey. If it weighed less than twenty pounds, he said, he'd eat it, feathers and all. He asked Laura, "How's that for a Christmas dinner? Think you can manage one of those drumsticks?"

She said, yes, she could. But she was sober. Then Mary asked him if the creek was going down, and he said it was still rising.

Ma said it was too bad. She hated to think of Mr. Edwards eating his bachelor cooking all alone on Christmas day. Mr. Edwards had been asked to eat Christmas dinner with them, but Pa shook his head and said a man would risk his neck, trying to cross that creek now.

"No," he said. "That current's too strong. We'll just have to make up our minds that Edwards won't be here tomorrow."

Of course that meant that Santa Claus could not come, either.

Laura and Mary tried not to mind too much. They watched Ma dress the wild turkey, and it was a very fat turkey. They were lucky little girls, to have a good house to live in, and a warm fire to sit by, and such a turkey for their Christmas dinner. Ma said so, and it was true. Ma said it was too bad that Santa Claus couldn't come this year, but they were such good girls that he hadn't forgotten them; he would surely come next year.

Still, they were not happy.

After supper that night they washed their hands and faces, buttoned their red-flannel night-gowns, tied their night-cap strings, and soberly said their prayers. They lay down in bed

and pulled the covers up. It did not seem at all like Christmas time.

Pa and Ma sat silently by the fire. After a while Ma asked why Pa didn't play the fiddle, and he said, "I don't seem to have the heart to, Caroline."

After a longer while, Ma suddenly stood up.

"I'm going to hang up your stockings, girls," she said. "Maybe something will happen."

Laura's heart jumped. But then she thought again of the creek and she knew nothing could happen.

Ma took one of Mary's clean stockings and one of Laura's, and she hung them from the mantel-shelf, on either side of the fireplace. Laura and Mary watched her over the edge of their bedcovers.

"Now go to sleep," Ma said, kissing them goodnight. "Morning will come quicker if you're asleep."

She sat down again by the fire and Laura almost went to sleep. She woke up a little when she heard Pa say, "You've only made it worse, Caroline." And she thought she heard Ma say: "No, Charles. There's the white sugar." But perhaps she was dreaming.

Then she heard Jack growl savagely. The door-latch rattled and some one said, "Ingalls! Ingalls!" Pa was stirring up the fire, and when he opened the door Laura saw that it was morning. The outdoors was gray.

"Great fishhooks, Edwards! Come in, man! What's happened?" Pa exclaimed.

Laura saw the stockings limply dangling, and she scrooged her shut eyes into the pillow. She heard Pa piling wood on the fire, and she heard Mr. Edwards say he had carried his clothes on his head when he swam the creek. His teeth rattled and his voice shivered. He would be all right, he said, as soon as he got warm.

"It was too big a risk, Edwards," Pa said. "We're glad you're here, but that was too big a risk for a Christmas dinner."

"Your little ones had to have a Christmas," Mr. Edwards replied. "No creek could stop me,

after I fetched them their gifts from Independence."

Laura sat straight up in bed. "Did you see Santa Claus?" she shouted.

"I sure did," Mr. Edwards said.

"Where? When? What did he look like? What did he say? Did he really give you something for us?" Mary and Laura cried.

"Wait, wait a minute!" Mr. Edwards laughed. And Ma said she would put the presents in the stockings, as Santa Claus intended. She said they mustn't look.

Mr. Edwards came and sat on the floor by their bed, and he answered every question they asked him. They honestly tried not to look at Ma, and they didn't quite see what she was doing.

When he saw the creek rising, Mr. Edwards said, he had known that Santa Claus could not get across it. ("But you crossed it," Laura said. "Yes," Mr. Edwards replied, "but Santa Claus is too old and fat. He couldn't make it, where a long, lean razor-back like me could do so.") And Mr. Edwards reasoned that if Santa Claus couldn't cross the creek, likely he would come no farther south than Independence. Why should he come forty miles across the prairie, only to be turned back? Of course he wouldn't do that!

So Mr. Edwards had walked to Independence. ("In the rain?" Mary asked. Mr. Edwards said he wore his rubber coat.) And there, coming down the street in Independence, he had met Santa Claus. ("In the daytime?" Laura asked. She hadn't thought that anyone could see Santa Claus in the daytime. No, Mr. Edwards said; it was night, but light shone out across the street from the saloons.)

Well, the first thing Santa Claus said was, "Hello, Edwards!" ("Did he know you?" Mary asked, and Laura asked, "How did you know he was really Santa Claus?" Mr. Edwards said that Santa Claus knew everybody. And he had recognized Santa at once by his whiskers. Santa Claus had the longest, thickest, whitest set of whiskers west of the Mississippi.)

So Santa Claus said, "Hello, Edwards! Last

time I saw you you were sleeping on a corn-shuck bed in Tennessee." And Mr. Edwards well remembered the little pair of red-yarn mittens that Santa Claus had left for him that time.

Then Santa Claus said: "I understand you're living now down along the Verdigris River. Have you ever met up, down yonder, with two little girls named Mary and Laura?"

"I surely am acquainted with them," Mr. Edwards replied.

"It rests heavy on my mind," said Santa Claus. "They are both of them sweet, pretty, good little young things, and I know they are expecting me. I surely do hate to disappoint two good little girls like them. Yet with the water up the way it is, I can't ever make it across that creek. I can figure no way whatsoever to get to their cabin this year. Edwards," Santa Claus said. "Would you do me the favor to fetch them their gifts one time?"

"I'll do that, and with pleasure," Mr. Edwards told him.

Then Santa Claus and Mr. Edwards stepped across the street to the hitching-posts where the pack-mule was tied. ("Didn't he have his reindeer?" Laura asked. "You know he couldn't," Mary said. "There isn't any snow." Exactly, said Mr. Edwards. Santa Claus traveled with a pack-mule in the southwest.)

And Santa Claus uncinched the pack and looked through it, and he took out the presents for Mary and Laura.

"Oh, what are they?" Laura cried; but Mary asked, "Then what did he do?"

Then he shook hands with Mr. Edwards, and he swung up on his fine bay horse. Santa Claus rode well, for a man of his weight and build. And he tucked his long, white whiskers under his bandana. "So long, Edwards," he said, and he rode away on the Fort Dodge trail, leading his pack-mule and whistling.

Laura and Mary were silent an instant, thinking of that.

Then Ma said, "You may look now, girls."

Something was shining bright in the top of Laura's stocking. She squealed and jumped out of bed. So did Mary, but Laura beat her to the fireplace. And the shining thing was a glittering new tin cup.

Mary had one exactly like it.

These new tin cups were their very own. Now they each had a cup to drink out of. Laura jumped up and down and shouted and laughed, but Mary stood still and looked with shining eyes at her own tin cup.

Then they plunged their hands into the stockings again. And they pulled out two long, long sticks of candy. It was peppermint candy, striped red and white. They looked and looked at that beautiful candy, and Laura licked her stick, just one lick. But Mary was not so greedy. She didn't take even one lick of her stick.

Those stockings weren't empty yet. Mary and Laura pulled out two small packages. They unwrapped them, and each found a little heart-shaped cake. Over their delicate brown tops was sprinkled white sugar. The sparkling grains lay like tiny drifts of snow.

The cakes were too pretty to eat. Mary and Laura just looked at them. But at last Laura turned hers over, and she nibbled a tiny nibble from underneath, where it wouldn't show. And the inside of that little cake was white!

It had been made of pure white flour, and sweetened with white sugar.

Laura and Mary never would have looked in their stockings again. The cups and the cakes and the candy were almost too much. They were too happy to speak. But Ma asked if they were sure the stockings were empty.

Then they put their arms down inside them, to make sure.

And in the very toe of each stocking was a shining bright, new penny!

They had never even thought of such a thing as having a penny. Think of having a whole penny for your very own. Think of having a cup and a cake and a stick of candy *and* a penny.

There never had been such a Christmas.

Now of course, right away, Laura and Mary should have thanked Mr. Edwards for bringing

those lovely presents all the way from Independence. But they had forgotten all about Mr. Edwards. They had even forgotten Santa Claus. In a minute they would have remembered, but before they did, Ma said, gently, "Aren't you going to thank Mr. Edwards?"

"Oh, thank you, Mr. Edwards! Thank you!" they said, and they meant it with all their hearts. Pa shook Mr. Edwards' hand, too, and shook it again. Pa and Ma and Mr. Edwards acted as if they were almost crying, Laura didn't know why. So she gazed again at her beautiful presents.

She looked up again when Ma gasped. And Mr. Edwards was taking sweet potatoes out of his pockets. He said they had helped to balance the package on his head when he swam across the creek. He thought Pa and Ma might like them, with the Christmas turkey.

There were nine sweet potatoes. Mr. Edwards had brought them all the way from town, too. It was just too much. Pa said so. "It's too much, Edwards," he said. They never could thank him enough.

Mary and Laura were too much excited to eat breakfast. They drank the milk from their shining new cups, but they could not swallow the rabbit stew and the cornmeal mush.

"Don't make them, Charles," Ma said. "It will soon be dinnertime."

For Christmas dinner there was the tender, juicy, roasted turkey. There were the sweet potatoes, baked in the ashes and carefully wiped so that you could eat the good skins, too. There was a loaf of salt-rising bread made from the last of the white flour.

And after all that there were stewed dried blackberries and little cakes. But these little cakes were made with brown sugar and they did not have white sugar sprinkled over their tops.

Then Pa and Ma and Mr. Edwards sat by the fire and talked about Christmas times back in Tennessee and up north in the Big Woods. But Mary and Laura looked at their beautiful cakes and played with their pennies and drank water out of their new cups. And little by little they licked and sucked their sticks of candy, till each stick was sharp-pointed on one end.

That was a happy Christmas.

One Christmas Eve

LANGSTON HUGHES

Standing over the hot stove cooking supper, the colored maid, Arcie, was very tired. Between meals today, she had cleaned the whole house for the white family she worked for, getting ready for Christmas tomorrow. Now her back ached and her head felt faint from sheer fatigue. Well, she would be off in a little while, if only the Missus and her children would come on home to dinner. They were out shopping for more things for the tree which stood all ready, tinsel-hung and lovely in the living-room, waiting for its candles to be lighted.

Arcie wished she could afford a tree for Joe. He'd never had one yet, and it's nice to have such things when you're little. Joe was five, going on six. Arcie, looking at the roast in the white folks' oven, wondered how much she could afford to spend tonight on toys. She only got seven dollars a week, and four of that went for her room and the landlady's daily looking after Joe while Arcie was at work.

"Lord, it's more'n a notion raisin' a child," she thought.

She looked at the clock on the kitchen table. After seven. What made white folks so darned inconsiderate? Why didn't they come on home here to supper? They knew she wanted to get off before all the stores closed. She wouldn't have time to buy Joe nothin' if they didn't hurry. And her landlady probably wanting to go out and shop, too, and not be bothered with little Joe.

"Dog gone it!" Arcie said to herself. "If I just had my money, I might leave the supper on the stove for 'em. I just got to get to the stores fo' they close." But she hadn't been paid for the week yet.

The Missus had promised to pay her Christmas Eve, a day or so ahead of time.

Arcie heard a door slam and talking and laughter in the front of the house. She went in and saw the Missus and her kids shaking snow off their coats.

"Umm-mm! It's swell for Christmas Eve," one of the kids said to Arcie. "It's snowin' like the deuce, and mother came near driving through a stop light. Can't hardly see for the snow. It's swell!"

"Supper's ready," Arcie said. She was thinking how her shoes weren't very good for walking in snow.

It seemed like the white folks took as long as they could to eat that evening. While Arcie was washing dishes, the Missus came out with her money.

"Arcie," the Missus said, "I'm so sorry, but would you mind if I just gave you five dollars tonight? The children have made me run short of change, buying presents and all."

"I'd like to have seven," Arcie said. "I needs it."

"Well, I just haven't got seven," the Missus said. "I didn't know you'd want all your money before the end of the week, anyhow. I just haven't got it to spare."

Arcie took five. Coming out of the hot kitchen, she wrapped up as well as she could and hurried by the house where she roomed to get little Joe. At least he could look at the Christmas trees in the windows downtown.

The landlady, a big light yellow woman, was in a bad humor. She said to Arcie, "I thought you

was comin' home early and get this child. I guess you know I want to go out, too, once in awhile."

Arcie didn't say anything for, if she had, she knew the landlady would probably throw it up to her that she wasn't getting paid to look after a child both night and day.

"Come on, Joe," Arcie said to her son, "let's us go in the street."

"I hears they got a Santa Claus down town," Joe said, wriggling into his worn little coat. "I wants to see him."

"Don't know 'bout that," his mother said, "but hurry up and get your rubbers on. Stores'll all be closed directly."

It was six or eight blocks downtown. They trudged along through the falling snow, both of them a little cold. But the snow was pretty!

The main street was hung with bright red and blue lights. In front of the City Hall there was a Christmas tree—but it didn't have no presents on it, only lights. In the store windows there were lots of toys—for sale.

Joe kept on saying, "Mama, I want . . ."

But mama kept walking ahead. It was nearly ten, when the stores were due to close, and Arcie wanted to get Joe some cheap gloves and something to keep him warm, as well as a toy or two. She thought she might come across a rummage sale where they had children's clothes. And in the ten-cent store, she could get some toys.

"O-oo! Lookee . . . ," little Joe kept saying, and pointing at things in the windows. How warm and pretty the lights were, and the shops, and the electric signs through the snow.

It took Arcie more than a dollar to get Joe's mittens and things he needed. In the A. & P. Arcie bought a big box of hard candies for 49c. And then she guided Joe through the crowd on the street until they came to the dime store. Near the ten-cent store they passed a moving picture theatre. Joe said he wanted to go in and see the movies.

Arcie said, "Ump-un! No, child! This ain't Baltimore where they have shows for colored, too. In these here small towns, they don't let colored folks in. We can't go in there."

"Oh," said little Joe.

In the ten-cent store, there was an awful crowd. Arcie told Joe to stand outside and wait for her. Keeping hold of him in the crowded store would be a job. Besides she didn't want him to see what toys she was buying. They were to be a surprise from Santa Claus tomorrow.

Little Joe stood outside the ten-cent store in the light, and the snow, and people passing. Gee, Christmas was pretty. All tinsel and stars and cotton. And Santa Claus a-coming from somewhere, dropping things in stockings. And all the people in the streets were carrying things, and the kids looked happy.

But Joe soon got tired of just standing and thinking and waiting in front of the ten-cent store. There were so many things to look at in the other windows. He moved along up the block a little, and then a little more, walking and looking. In fact, he moved until he came to the white folks' picture show.

In the lobby of the moving picture show, behind the plate glass doors, it was all warm and glowing and awful pretty. Joe stood looking in, and as he looked his eyes began to make out, in there blazing beneath holly and colored streamers and the electric stars of the lobby, a marvellous Christmas tree. A group of children and grown-ups, white, of course, were standing around a big jovial man in red beside the tree. Or was it a man? Little Joe's eyes opened wide. No, it was not a man at all. It was Santa Claus!

Little Joe pushed open one of the glass doors and ran into the lobby of the white moving picture show. Little Joe went right through the crowd and up to where he could get a good look at Santa Claus. And Santa Claus was giving away gifts, little presents for children, little boxes of animal crackers and stick-candy canes. And behind him on the tree was a big sign (which little Joe didn't know how to read). It said, to those who understood, MERRY XMAS FROM SANTA CLAUS TO OUR YOUNG PATRONS.

Around the lobby, other signs said, WHEN

YOU COME OUT OF THE SHOW STOP WITH YOUR CHILDREN AND SEE OUR SANTA CLAUS. And another announced, GEM THEATRE MAKES ITS CUSTOMERS HAPPY—SEE OUR SANTA.

And there was Santa Claus in a red suit and a white beard all sprinkled with tinsel snow. Around him were rattles and drums and rocking horses which he was not giving away. But the signs on them said (could little Joe have read) that they would be presented from the stage on Christmas Day to the holders of the lucky numbers. Tonight, Santa Claus was only giving away candy, and stick-candy canes, and animal crackers to the kids.

Joe would have liked terribly to have a stick-candy cane. He came a little closer to Santa Claus, until he was right in the front of the crowd. And then Santa Claus saw Joe.

Why is it that lots of white people always grin when they see a Negro child? Santa Claus grinned. Everybody else grinned, too, looking at little black Joe—who had no business in the lobby of a white theatre. Then Santa Claus stooped down and slyly picked up one of his lucky number rattles, a great big loud tin-pan rattle such as they use in cabarets. And he shook it fiercely right at Joe. That was funny. The white people laughed, kids and all. But little Joe didn't laugh. He was scared. To the shaking of the big rattle, he turned and fled out of the warm lobby of the theatre, out into the street where the snow

was and the people. Frightened by laughter, he had begun to cry. He went looking for his mama. In his heart he never thought Santa Claus shook great rattles at children like that—and then laughed.

In the crowd on the street he went the wrong way. He couldn't find the ten-cent store or his mother. There were too many people, all white people, moving like white shadows in the snow, a world of white people.

It seemed to Joe an awfully long time till he suddenly saw Arcie, dark and worried-looking, cut across the side-walk through the passing crowd and grab him. Although her arms were full of packages, she still managed with one free hand to shake him until his teeth rattled.

"Why didn't you stand where I left you?" Arcie demanded loudly. "Tired as I am, I got to run all over the streets in the night lookin' for you. I'm a great mind to wear you out."

When little Joe got his breath back, on the way home, he told his mama he had been in the moving picture show.

"But Santa Claus didn't give me nothin'," Joe said tearfully. "He made a big noise at me and I runned out."

"Serves you right," said Arcie, trudging through the snow. "You had no business in there. I told you to stay where I left you."

"But I seed Santa Claus in there," little Joe said, "so I went in."

"Huh! That wasn't no Santa Claus," Arcie explained. "If it was, he wouldn't a-treated you like that. That's a theatre for white folks—I told you once—and he's just a old white man."

"Oh . . . ," said little Joe.

Christmas Every Day

WILLIAM DEAN HOWELLS

The little girl came into her papa's study, as she always did Saturday morning before breakfast, and asked for a story. He tried to beg off that morning, for he was very busy, but she would not let him. So he began:

"Well, once there was a little pig—"

She put her hand over his mouth and stopped him at the word. She said she had heard little pig stories till she was perfectly sick of them.

"Well, what kind of story *shall* I tell, then?"

"About Christmas. It's getting to be the season. It's past Thanksgiving already."

"It seems to me," argued her papa, "that I've told as often about Christmas as I have about little pigs."

"No difference! Christmas is more interesting."

"Well!" Her papa roused himself from his writing by a great effort. "Well, then, I'll tell you about the little girl that wanted it Christmas every day in the year. How would you like that?"

"First-rate!" said the little girl; and she nestled into comfortable shape in his lap, ready for listening.

"Very well, then, this little pig—Oh, what are you pounding me for?"

"Because you said little pig instead of little girl."

"I should like to know what's the difference between a little pig and a little girl that wanted it Christmas every day!"

"Papa," said the little girl, warningly, "if you don't go on, I'll *give* it to you!" And at this her papa darted off like lightning, and began to tell the story as fast as he could.

Well, once there was a little girl who liked Christmas so much that she wanted it to be Christmas every day in the year; and as soon as Thanksgiving was over she began to send postal cards to the old Christmas Fairy to ask if she mightn't have it. But the old Fairy never answered any of the postals; and, after a while, the little girl found out that the Fairy was pretty particular, and wouldn't even notice anything but letters, not even correspondence cards in envelopes; but real letters on sheets of paper, and sealed outside with a monogram—or your initial, any way. So, then, she began to send her letters; and in about three weeks—or just the day before Christmas, it was—she got a letter from the Fairy, saying she might have it Christmas every day for a year, and then they would see about having it longer.

The little girl was a good deal excited already, preparing for the old-fashioned, once-a-year Christmas that was coming the next day, and perhaps the Fairy's promise didn't make such an impression on her as it would have made at some other time. She just resolved to keep it to herself, and surprise everybody with it as it kept coming true; and then it slipped out of her mind altogether.

She had a splendid Christmas. She went to bed early, so as to let Santa Claus have a chance at the stockings, and in the morning she was up the first of anybody and went and felt them, and found hers all lumpy with packages of candy, and oranges and grapes, and pocket-books and rubber balls and all kinds of small presents, and her big brother's with nothing but the tongs in them, and

her young lady sister's with a new silk umbrella, and her papa's and mamma's with potatoes and pieces of coal wrapped up in tissue paper, just as they always had every Christmas. Then she waited around till the rest of the family were up, and she was the first to burst into the library, when the doors were opened, and look at the large presents laid out on the library-table—books, and portfolios, and boxes of stationery, and breast-pins, and dolls, and little stoves, and dozens of handkerchiefs, and ink-stands, and skates, and snow-shovels, and photograph-frames, and little easels, and boxes of water-colors, and Turkish paste, and nougat, and candied cherries, and dolls' houses, and water-proofs—and the big Christmas-tree, lighted and standing in a waste-basket in the middle.

She had a splendid Christmas all day. She ate so much candy that she did not want any break-fast; and the whole forenoon the presents kept pouring in that the expressman had not had time to deliver the night before; and she went 'round giving the presents she had got for other people, and came home and ate turkey and cranberry for dinner, and plum-pudding and nuts and raisins and oranges and more candy, and then went out and coasted and came in with a stomach-ache, crying; and her papa said he would see if his house was turned into that sort of fool's paradise another year; and they had a light supper, and pretty early everybody went to bed cross.

Here the little girl pounded her papa in the back, again.

"Well, what now? Did I say pigs?"

"You made them *act* like pigs."

"Well, didn't they?"

"No matter; you oughtn't to put it into a story."

"Very well, then, I'll take it all out."

Her father went on:

The little girl slept very heavily, and she slept very late, but she was wakened at last by the other children dancing 'round her bed with their stockings full of presents in their hands.

"What is it?" said the little girl, and she rubbed her eyes and tried to rise up in bed.

"Christmas! Christmas! Christmas!" they all shouted, and waved their stockings.

"Nonsense! It was Christmas yesterday."

Her brothers and sisters just laughed. "We don't know about that. It's Christmas to-day, any way. You come into the library and see."

Then all at once it flashed on the little girl that the Fairy was keeping her promise, and her year of Christmases was beginning. She was dreadfully sleepy, but she sprang up like a lark—a lark that had overeaten itself and gone to bed cross—and darted into the library. There it was again! Books, and portfolios, and boxes of stationery, and breast-pins—

"You needn't go over it all, Papa; I guess I can remember just what was there," said the little girl.

Well, and there was the Christmas-tree blazing away, and the family picking out their presents, but looking pretty sleepy, and her father perfectly puzzled, and her mother ready to cry. "I'm sure I don't see how I'm to dispose of all these things," said her mother, and her father said it seemed to him they had had something just like it the day before, but he supposed he must have dreamed it. This struck the little girl as the best kind of joke; and so she ate so much candy she didn't want any breakfast, and went 'round carrying presents, and had turkey and cranberry for dinner, and then went out and coasted, and came in with a—

"Papa!"

"Well, what now?"

"What did you promise, you forgetful thing?"

"Oh! oh, yes!"

Well, the next day, it was just the same thing over again, but everybody getting crosser; and at the end of a week's time so many people had lost their tempers that you could pick up lost tempers everywhere; they perfectly strewed the ground. Even when people tried to recover their tempers

they usually got somebody else's, and it made the most dreadful mix.

The little girl began to get frightened, keeping the secret all to herself; she wanted to tell her mother, but she didn't dare to; and she was ashamed to ask the Fairy to take back her gift, it seemed ungrateful and ill-bred, and she thought she would try to stand it, but she hardly knew how she could, for a whole year. So it went on and on, and it was Christmas on St. Valentine's Day, and Washington's Birthday just the same as any day, and it didn't skip even the First of April, though everything was counterfeit that day, and that was some *little* relief.

After a while, coal and potatoes began to be awfully scarce, so many had been wrapped up in tissue paper to fool papas and mammas with. Turkeys got to be about a thousand dollars apiece—

"Papa!"
"Well, what?"
"You're beginning to fib."
"Well, *two* thousand, then."

And they got to passing off almost anything for turkeys—half-grown humming-birds, and even rocs out of the "Arabian Nights"—the real turkeys were so scarce. And cranberries—well, they asked a diamond apiece for cranberries. All the woods and orchards were cut down for Christmas-trees, and where the woods and orchards used to be, it looked just like a stubble-field, with the stumps. After a while they had to make Christmas-trees out of rags, and stuff them with bran, like old-fashioned dolls; but there were plenty of rags, because people got so poor, buying presents for one another, that they couldn't get any new clothes, and they just wore their old ones to tatters. They got so poor that everybody had to go to the poor-house, except the confectioners, and the fancy store-keepers, and the picture-booksellers, and the expressmen; and *they* all got so rich and proud that they would hardly wait upon a person when he came to buy; it was perfectly shameful!

Well, after it had gone on about three or four months, the little girl, whenever she came into the room in the morning and saw those great ugly lumpy stockings dangling at the fire-place, and the disgusting presents around everywhere, used to just sit down and burst out crying. In six months she was perfectly exhausted; she couldn't even cry any more; she just lay on the lounge and rolled her eyes and panted. About the beginning of October she took to sitting down on dolls, wherever she found them—French dolls, or any kind—she hated the sight of them so; and by Thanksgiving she was crazy, and just slammed her presents across the room.

By that time people didn't carry presents around nicely any more. They flung them over the fence, or through the window, or anything; and, instead of running their tongues out and taking great pains to write "For dear Papa," or "Mamma," or "Brother," or "Sister," or "Susie," or "Sammie," or "Billie," or "Bobby," or "Jimmie," or "Jennie," or whoever it was, and troubling to get the spelling right, and then signing their names, and "'Xmas, 188—," they used to write in the gift-books, "Take it, you horrid old thing!" and then go and bang it against the front door. Nearly everybody had built barns to hold their presents, but pretty soon the barns overflowed, and then they used to let them lie out in the rain, or anywhere. Sometimes the police used to come and tell them to shovel their presents off the sidewalk, or they would arrest them.

"I thought you said everybody had gone to the poor-house," interrupted the little girl.

"They did go, at first," said her papa; "but after a while the poor-houses got so full that they had to send the people back to their own houses. They tried to cry, when they got back, but they couldn't make the least sound."

"Why couldn't they?"

"Because they had lost their voices, saying 'Merry Christmas' so much. Did I tell you how it was on the Fourth of July?"

"No; how was it?" And the little girl nestled closer, in expectation of something uncommon.

Well, the night before, the boys stayed up to celebrate, as they always do, and fell asleep before twelve o'clock, as usual, expecting to be wakened by the bells and cannon. But it was nearly eight o'clock before the first boy in the United States woke up, and then he found out what the trouble was. As soon as he could get his clothes on, he ran out of the house and smashed a big cannon-torpedo down on the pavement; but it didn't make any more noise than a damp wad of paper, and, after he tried about twenty or thirty more, he began to pick them up and look at them. Every single torpedo was a big raisin! Then he just streaked it upstairs, and examined his fire-crackers and toy-pistol and two-dollar collection of fireworks and found that they were nothing but sugar and candy painted up to look like fireworks! Before ten o'clock, every boy in the United States found out that his Fourth of July things had turned into Christmas things; and then they just sat down and cried—they were so mad. There are about twenty million boys in the United States, and so you can imagine what a noise they made. Some men got together before night, with a little powder that hadn't turned into purple sugar yet, and they said they would fire off *one* cannon, any way. But the cannon burst into a thousand pieces, for it was nothing but rock-candy, and some of the men nearly got killed. The Fourth of July orations all turned into Christmas carols, and when anybody tried to read the Declaration, instead of saying, "When in the course of human events it becomes necessary," he was sure to sing, "God rest you, merry gentlemen." It was perfectly awful.

The little girl drew a deep sigh of satisfaction . "And how was it at Thanksgiving?" she asked. Her papa hesitated. "Well, I'm almost afraid to tell you. I'm afraid you'll think it's wicked." "Well, tell, any way," said the little girl.

Well, before it came Thanksgiving, it had leaked out who had caused all these Christmases. The little girl had suffered so much that she had talked about it in her sleep; and after that, hardly anybody would play with her. People just perfectly despised her, because if it had not been for her greediness, it wouldn't have happened; and now, when it came Thanksgiving, and she wanted them to go to church, and have a squash-pie and turkey, and show their gratitude, they said that all the turkeys had been eaten up for her old Christmas dinners, and if she would stop the Christmases, they would see about the gratitude. Wasn't it dreadful? And the very next day the little girl began to send letters to the Christmas Fairy, and then telegrams, to stop it. But it didn't do any good; and then she got to calling at the Fairy's house, but the girl that came to the door always said "Not at home," or "Engaged," or "At

dinner," or something like that; and so it went on till it came the old once-a-year Christmas Eve. The little girl fell asleep, and when she woke up in the morning—

"She found it was all nothing but a dream," suggested the little girl.

"No, indeed!" said her papa. "It was all every bit true!"

"Well, what *did* she find out then?"

"Why, that it wasn't Christmas at last, and wasn't ever going to be, any more. Now it's time for breakfast."

The little girl held her papa fast around the neck.

"You shan't go if you're going to leave it *so!*"

"How do you want it left?"

"Christmas once a year."

"All right," said her papa; and he went on again.

Well, there was the greatest rejoicing all over the country, and it extended clear up into Canada. The people met together everywhere, and kissed and cried for joy. The city carts went around and gathered up all the candy and raisins and nuts, and dumped them into the river; and it made the fish perfectly sick; and the whole United States, as far out as Alaska, was one blaze of bonfires, where the children were burning up their gift-books and presents of all kinds. They had the greatest *time!*

The little girl went to thank the old Fairy because she had stopped it being Christmas, and she said she hoped she would keep her promise, and see that Christmas never, never came again. Then the Fairy frowned, and asked her if she was sure she knew what she meant; and the little girl asked her, why not? and the old Fairy said that now she was behaving just as greedily as ever, and she'd better look out. This made the little girl think it all over carefully again, and she said she would be willing to have it Christmas about once in a thousand years; and then she said a hundred, and then she said ten, and at last she got down to one. Then the Fairy said that was the good old way that had pleased people ever since Christmas

began, and she was agreed. Then the little girl said, "What're your shoes made of?" And the Fairy said, "Leather." And the little girl said, "Bargain's done forever," and skipped off, and hippity-hopped the whole way home, she was so glad.

"How will that do?" asked the papa.

"First-rate!" said the little girl; but she hated to have the story stop, and was rather sober. However, her mamma put her head in at the door, and asked her papa:

"Are you never coming to breakfast? What have you been telling that child?"

"Oh, just a moral tale."

The little girl caught him around the neck again.

"*We* know! Don't you tell *what*, Papa! Don't you tell *what!*"

The Gift of the Magi

O. HENRY

One dollar and eighty-seven cents. That was all. And sixty cents of it was in pennies. Pennies saved one and two at a time by bulldozing the grocer and the vegetable man and the butcher until one's cheeks burned with the silent imputation of parsimony that such close dealing implied. Three times Della counted it. One dollar and eighty-seven cents. And the next day would be Christmas.

There was clearly nothing to do but flop down on the shabby little couch and howl. So Della did it. Which instigates the moral reflection that life is made up of sobs, sniffles, and smiles, with sniffles predominating.

While the mistress of the home is gradually subsiding from the first stage to the second, take a look at the home. A furnished flat at $8 per week. It did not exactly beggar description, but it certainly had that word on the lookout for the mendicancy squad.

In the vestibule below was a letter-box into which no letter would go, and an electric button from which no mortal finger could coax a ring. Also appertaining thereunto was a card bearing the name "Mr. James Dillingham Young."

The "Dillingham" had been flung to the breeze during a former period of prosperity when its possessor was being paid $30 per week. Now, when the income was shrunk to $20, the letters of "Dillingham" looked blurred, as though they were thinking seriously of contracting to a modest and unassuming D. But whenever Mr. James Dillingham Young came home and reached his flat above he was called "Jim" and greatly hugged by Mrs. James Dillingham Young, already introduced to you as Della. Which is all very good.

Della finished her cry and attended to her cheeks with the powder rag. She stood by the window and looked out dully at a grey cat walking a grey fence in a grey backyard. To-morrow would be Christmas Day, and she had only $1.87 with which to buy Jim a present. She had been saving every penny she could for months, with this result. Twenty dollars a week doesn't go far. Expenses had been greater than she had calculated. They always are. Only $1.87 to buy a present for Jim. Her Jim. Many a happy hour she had spent planning for something nice for him. Something fine and rare and sterling—something just a little bit near to being worthy of the honour of being owned by Jim.

There was a pier-glass between the windows of the room. Perhaps you have seen a pier-glass in an $8 flat. A very thin and very agile person may, by observing his reflection in a rapid sequence of longitudinal strips, obtain a fairly accurate conception of his looks. Della, being slender, had mastered the art.

Suddenly she whirled from the window and stood before the glass. Her eyes were shining brilliantly, but her face had lost its colour within twenty seconds. Rapidly she pulled down her hair and let it fall to its full length.

Now, there were two possessions of the James Dillingham Youngs in which they both took a mighty pride. One was Jim's gold watch that had been his father's and grandfather's. The other was Della's hair. Had the Queen of Sheba lived in the flat across the airshaft, Della would have let her hair hang out the window some day to dry just to depreciate Her Majesty's jewels and gifts. Had King Solomon been the janitor, with all his

treasures piled up in the basement, Jim would have pulled out his watch every time he passed, just to see him pluck at his beard from envy.

So now Della's beautiful hair fell about her, rippling and shining like a cascade of brown waters. It reached below her knee and made itself almost a garment for her. And then she did it up again nervously and quickly. Once she faltered for a minute and stood still while a tear or two splashed on the worn red carpet.

On went her old brown jacket; on went her old brown hat. With a whirl of skirts and with the brilliant sparkle still in her eyes, she fluttered out the door and down the stairs to the street.

Where she stopped the sign read: "Mme. Sofronie. Hair Goods of All Kinds." One flight up Della ran, and collected herself, panting. Madame, large, too white, chilly, hardly looked the "Sofronie."

"Will you buy my hair?" asked Della.

"I buy hair," said Madame. "Take yer hat off and let's have a sight at the looks of it."

Down rippled the brown cascade.

"Twenty dollars," said Madame, lifting the mass with a practised hand.

"Give it to me quick," said Della.

Oh, and the next two hours tripped by on rosy wings. Forget the hashed metaphor. She was ransacking the stores for Jim's present.

She found it at last. It surely had been made for Jim and no one else. There was no other like it in any of the stores, and she had turned all of them inside out. It was a platinum fob chain simple and chaste in design, properly proclaiming its value by substance alone and not by meretricious ornamentation—as all good things should do. It was even worthy of The Watch. As soon as she saw it she knew that it must be Jim's. It was like him. Quietness and value—the description applied to both. Twenty-one dollars they took from her for it, and she hurried home with the 87 cents. With that chain on his watch Jim might be properly anxious about the time in any company. Grand as the watch was, he sometimes looked at it on the sly on account of the old leather strap that he used in place of a chain.

When Della reached home her intoxication gave way a little to prudence and reason. She got out her curling irons and lighted the gas and went to work repairing the ravages made by generosity added to love. Which is always a tremendous task, dear friends—a mammoth task.

Within forty minutes her head was covered with tiny close-lying curls that made her look wonderfully like a truant schoolboy. She looked at her reflection in the mirror long, carefully, and critically.

"If Jim doesn't kill me," she said to herself, "before he takes a second look at me, he'll say I look like a Coney Island chorus girl. But what could I do—oh! what could I do with a dollar and eighty-seven cents?"

At 7 o'clock the coffee was made and the frying-pan was on the back of the stove hot and ready to cook the chops.

Jim was never late. Della doubled the fob chain in her hand and sat on the corner of the table near the door that he always entered. Then she heard his step on the stair away down on the first flight, and she turned white for just a moment. She had a habit of saying little silent prayers about the simplest everyday things, and now she whispered: "Please God, make him think I am still pretty."

The door opened and Jim stepped in and closed it. He looked thin and very serious. Poor fellow, he was only twenty-two—and to be burdened with a family! He needed a new overcoat and he was without gloves.

Jim stopped inside the door, as immovable as a setter at the scent of quail. His eyes were fixed upon Della, and there was an expression in them that she could not read, and it terrified her. It was not anger, nor surprise, nor disapproval, nor horror, nor any of the sentiments that she had been prepared for. He simply stared at her fixedly with that peculiar expression on his face.

Della wriggled off the table and went for him.

"Jim, darling," she cried, "don't look at me that way. I had my hair cut off and sold it because I couldn't have lived through Christmas without giving you a present. It'll grow out again—you won't mind, will you? I just had to do it. My hair

grows awfully fast. Say 'Merry Christmas!' Jim, and let's be happy. You don't know what a nice—what a beautiful, nice gift I've got for you."

"You've cut off your hair?" asked Jim, laboriously, as if he had not arrived at that patent fact yet even after the hardest mental labour.

"Cut it off and sold it," said Della. "Don't you like me just as well, anyhow? I'm me without my hair, ain't I?"

Jim looked about the room curiously.

"You say your hair is gone?" he said, with an air almost of idiocy.

"You needn't look for it," said Della. "It's sold, I tell you—sold and gone, too. It's Christmas Eve, boy. Be good to me, for it went for you. Maybe the hairs of my head were numbered," she went on with a sudden serious sweetness, "but nobody could ever count my love for you. Shall I put the chops on, Jim?"

Out of his trance Jim seemed quickly to wake. He enfolded his Della. For ten seconds let us regard with discreet scrutiny some inconsequential object in the other direction. Eight dollars a week or a million a year—what is the difference? A mathematician or a wit would give you the wrong answer. The magi brought valuable gifts, but that was not among them. This dark assertion will be illuminated later on.

Jim drew a package from his overcoat pocket and threw it upon the table.

"Don't make any mistake, Dell," he said, "about me. I don't think there's anything in the way of a haircut or a shave or a shampoo that could make me like my girl any less. But if you'll unwrap that package you may see why you had me going a while at first."

White fingers and nimble tore at the string and paper. And then an ecstatic scream of joy; and then, alas! a quick feminine change to hysterical tears and wails, necessitating the immediate employment of all the comforting powers of the lord of the flat.

For there lay The Combs—the set of combs, side and back, that Della had worshipped for long in a Broadway window. Beautiful combs, pure tortoise shell, with jeweled rims—just the shade to wear in the beautiful vanished hair. They were expensive combs, she knew, and her heart had simply craved and yearned over them without the least hope of possession. And now, they were hers, but the tresses that should have adorned the coveted adornments were gone.

But she hugged them to her bosom, and at length she was able to look up with dim eyes and a smile and say: "My hair grows so fast, Jim!"

And then Della leaped up like a little singed cat and cried, "Oh, oh!"

Jim had not yet seen his beautiful present. She held it out to him eagerly upon her open palm. The dull precious metal seemed to flash with a reflection of her bright and ardent spirit.

"Isn't it a dandy, Jim? I hunted all over town to find it. You'll have to look at the time a hundred times a day now. Give me your watch. I want to see how it looks on it."

Instead of obeying, Jim tumbled down on the couch and put his hands under the back of his head and smiled.

"Dell," said he, "let's put our Christmas presents away and keep 'em a while. They're too nice to use just at present. I sold the watch to get the money to buy your combs. And now suppose you put the chops on."

The magi, as you know, were wise men—wonderfully wise men who brought gifts to the Babe in the manger. They invented the art of giving Christmas presents. Being wise, their gifts were no doubt wise ones, possibly bearing the privilege of exchange in case of duplication. And here I have lamely related to you the uneventful chronicle of two foolish children in a flat who most unwisely sacrificed for each other the greatest treasures of their house. But in a last word to the wise of these days let it be said that of all who give gifts these two were the wisest. Of all who give and receive gifts, such as they are wisest. Everywhere they are wisest. They are the magi.

The Story of the Goblins Who Stole a Sexton

CHARLES DICKENS

"In an old abbey town, down in this part of the country, a long, long while ago—so long, that the story must be a true one, because our great grandfathers implicitly believed it—there officiated as sexton and grave-digger in the churchyard, one Gabriel Grub. It by no means follows that because a man is a sexton, and constantly surrounded by the emblems of mortality, therefore he should be a morose and melancholy man; your undertakers are the merriest fellows in the world; and I once had the honour of being on intimate terms with a mute, who in private life, and off duty, was as comical and jocose a little fellow as ever chirped out a devil-may-care song, without a hitch in his memory, or drained off the contents of a good stiff glass without stopping for breath. But, notwithstanding these precedents to the contrary, Gabriel Grub was an ill-conditioned, cross-grained, surly fellow—a morose and lonely man, who consorted with nobody but himself, and an old wicker bottle which fitted into his large deep waistcoat pocket—and who eyed each merry face, as it passed him by, with such a deep scowl of malice and ill-humour, as it was difficult to meet, without feeling something the worse for.

"A little before twilight, one Christmas eve, Gabriel shouldered his spade, lighted his lantern, and betook himself towards the old churchyard; for he had got a grave to finish by next morning, and, feeling very low, he thought it might raise his spirits, perhaps, if he went on with his work at once. As he went his way, up the ancient street, he saw the cheerful light of the blazing fires gleam through the old casements, and heard the loud laugh and the cheerful shouts of those who were assembled around them; he marked the bustling preparations for next day's cheer, and smelt the numerous savoury odours consequent thereupon, as they steamed up from the kitchen windows in clouds. All this was gall and wormwood to the heart of Gabriel Grub; and when groups of children bounded out of the houses, tripped across the road, and were met, before they could knock at the opposite door, by half a dozen curly-headed little rascals who crowded round them as they flocked up-stairs to spend the evening in their Christmas games, Gabriel smiled grimly, and clutched the handle of his spade with a firmer grasp, as he thought of measles, scarlet-fever, thrush, whooping-cough, and a good many other sources of consolation besides.

"In this happy frame of mind, Gabriel strode along: returning a short, sullen growl to the good-humoured greetings of such of his neighbours as now and then passed him: until he turned into the dark lane which led to the churchyard. Now, Gabriel had been looking forward to reaching the dark lane, because it was, generally speaking, a nice, gloomy, mournful place, into which the towns-people did not much care to go, except in broad daylight, and when the sun was shining; consequently, he was not a little indignant to hear a young urchin roaring out some jolly song about a merry Christmas, in this very sanctuary, which had been called Coffin Lane ever since the days of the old abbey, and the time of the shaven-headed monks. As Gabriel walked on, and the voice drew nearer, he found it proceeded from a small boy, who was hurrying along, to join one of the little parties in the old street, and who, partly to keep himself company, and partly to prepare himself for the occasion, was shouting out the song at the highest pitch of

his lungs. So Gabriel waited until the boy came up, and then dodged him into a corner, and rapped him over the head with his lantern five or six times, to teach him to modulate his voice. And as the boy hurried away with his hand to his head, singing quite a different sort of tune, Gabriel Grub chuckled very heartily to himself, and entered the churchyard: locking the gate behind him.

"He took off his coat, put down his lantern, and getting into the unfinished grave, worked at it for an hour or so, with right good will. But the earth was hardened with the frost, and it was no very easy matter to break it up, and shovel it out; and although there was a moon, it was a very young one, and shed little light upon the grave, which was in the shadow of the church. At any other time, these obstacles would have made Gabriel Grub very moody and miserable, but he was so well pleased with having stopped the small boy's singing, that he took little heed of the scanty progress he had made, and looked down into the grave, when he had finished work for the night, with grim satisfaction: murmuring as he gathered up his things:

Brave lodgings for one, brave lodgings for one,
A few feet of cold earth, when life is done;
A stone at the head, a stone at the feet,
A rich, juicy meal for the worms to eat;
Rank grass overhead, and damp clay around,
Brave lodgings for one, these, in holy ground!

"'Ho! ho!' laughed Gabriel Grub, as he sat himself down on a flat tombstone which was a favourite resting-place of his; and drew forth his wicker bottle. 'A coffin at Christmas! A Christmas Box. Ho! ho! ho!'

"'Ho! ho! ho!' repeated a voice which sounded close behind him.

"Gabriel paused in some alarm, in the act of raising the wicker bottle to his lips; and looked round. The bottom of the oldest grave about him, was not more still and quiet, than the churchyard in the pale moonlight. The cold hoarfrost glistened on the tombstones, and sparkled like rows of gems, among the stone carvings of the old church. The snow lay hard and crisp upon the ground; and spread over the thickly strewn mounds of earth so white and smooth a cover that it seemed as if corpses lay there, hidden only by their winding sheets. Not the faintest rustle broke the profound tranquillity of the solemn scene. Sound itself appeared to be frozen up, all was so cold and still.

"'It was the echoes,' said Gabriel Grub, raising the bottle to his lips again.

"'It was *not*,' said a deep voice.

"Gabriel started up, and stood rooted to the spot with astonishment and terror; for his eyes rested on a form that made his blood run cold.

"Seated on an upright tombstone, close to him, was a strange unearthly figure, whom Gabriel felt at once, was no being of this world. His long fantastic legs which might have reached the ground, were cocked up, and crossed after a quaint, fantastic fashion; his sinewy arms were bare; and his hands rested on his knees. On his short round body, he wore a close covering, ornamented with small slashes; a short cloak dangled at his back; the collar was cut into curious peaks, which served the goblin in lieu of ruff or neckerchief; and his shoes curled up at his toes into long points. On his head, he wore a broad-brimmed sugar-loaf hat, garnished with a single feather. The hat was covered with the white frost; and the goblin looked as if he had sat on the same tombstone very comfortably, for two or three hundred years. He was sitting perfectly still; his tongue was put out, as if in derision; and he was grinning at Gabriel Grub with such a grin as only a goblin could call up.

"'It was *not* the echoes,' said the goblin.

"Gabriel Grub was paralysed, and could make no reply.

"'What do you do here on Christmas eve?' said the goblin sternly.

"'I came to dig a grave, sir,' stammered Gabriel Grub.

"'What man wanders among graves and churchyards on such a night as this?' cried the goblin.

"'Gabriel Grub! Gabriel Grub!' screamed a

wild chorus of voices that seemed to fill the churchyard. Gabriel looked fearfully round—nothing was to be seen.

"'What have you got in that bottle?' said the goblin.

"'Hollands, sir,' replied the sexton, trembling more than ever; for he had bought it of the smugglers, and he thought that perhaps his questioner might be in the excise department of the goblins.

"'Who drinks Hollands alone, and in a churchyard, on such a night as this?' said the goblin.

"'Gabriel Grub! Gabriel Grub!' exclaimed the wild voices again.

"The goblin leered maliciously at the terrified sexton, and then raising his voice, exclaimed:

"'And who, then, is our fair and lawful prize?'

"To this inquiry the invisible chorus replied, in a strain that sounded like the voices of many choristers singing to the mighty swell of the old church organ—a strain that seemed borne to the

Norman Rockwell

sexton's ears upon a wild wind, and to die away as it passed onward; but the burden of the reply was still the same, 'Gabriel Grub! Gabriel Grub!'

"The goblin grinned a broader grin than before, as he said, 'Well, Gabriel, what do you say to this?'

"The sexton gasped for breath.

"'What do you think of this, Gabriel?' said the goblin, kicking up his feet in the air on either side of the tombstone, and looking at the turned-up points with as much complacency as if he had been contemplating the most fashionable pair of Wellingtons in all Bond Street.

"'It's—it's—very curious, sir,' replied the sexton, half dead with fright; 'very curious, and very pretty, but I think I'll go back and finish my work, sir, if you please.'

"'Work!' said the goblin, 'what work?'

"'The grave, sir; making the grave,' stammered the sexton.

"'Oh, the grave, eh?' said the goblin; 'who makes graves at a time when all other men are merry, and takes a pleasure in it?'

"Again the mysterious voices replied, 'Gabriel Grub! Gabriel Grub!'

"'I'm afraid my friends want you, Gabriel,' said the goblin, thrusting his tongue further into his cheek than ever—and a most astonishing tongue it was—'I'm afraid my friends want you, Gabriel,' said the goblin.

"'Under favour, sir,' replied the horror-stricken sexton, 'I don't think they can, sir; they don't know me, sir; I don't think the gentlemen have ever seen me, sir.'

"'Oh yes, they have,' replied the goblin; 'we know the man with the sulky face and grim scowl,

that came down the street to-night, throwing his evil looks at the children, and grasping his burying spade the tighter. We know the man who struck the boy in the envious malice of his heart, because the boy could be merry, and he could not. We know him, we know him.'

"Here, the goblin gave a loud shrill laugh, which the echoes returned twenty-fold: and throwing his legs up in the air, stood upon his head, or rather upon the very point of his sugar-loaf hat, on the narrow edge of the tombstone: whence he threw a somerset with extraordinary agility, right to the sexton's feet, at which he planted himself in the attitude in which tailors generally sit upon the shopboard.

"'I—I—am afraid I must leave you, sir,' said the sexton, making an effort to move.

"'Leave us!' said the goblin, 'Gabriel Grub going to leave us. Ho! ho! ho!'

"As the goblin laughed, the sexton observed, for one instant, a brilliant illumination within the windows of the church, as if the whole building were lighted up; it disappeared, the organ pealed forth a lively air, and whole troops of goblins, the very counterpart of the first one, poured into the churchyard, and began playing at leap-frog with the tombstones: never stopping for an instant to take breath, but 'overing' the highest among them, one after the other, with the most marvellous dexterity. The first goblin was a most astonishing leaper, and none of the others could come near him; even in the extremity of his terror the sexton could not help observing, that while his friends were content to leap over the common-sized gravestones, the first one took the family vaults, iron railings and all, with as much ease as if they had been so many street posts. At last the game reached to a most exciting pitch; the organ played quicker and quicker; and the goblins leaped faster and faster: coiling themselves up, rolling head over heels upon the ground, and bounding over the tombstones like foot-balls. The sexton's brain whirled round with the rapidity of the motion he beheld, and his legs reeled beneath him, as the spirits flew before his eyes: when the goblin king, suddenly darting towards him, laid his hand upon his collar, and sank with him through the earth.

"When Gabriel Grub had had time to fetch his breath, which the rapidity of his descent had for the moment taken away, he found himself in what appeared to be a large cavern, surrounded on all sides by crowds of goblins, ugly and grim; in the centre of the room, on an elevated seat, was stationed his friend of the churchyard; and close beside him stood Gabriel Grub himself, without power of motion.

"'Cold to-night,' said the king of goblins, 'very cold. A glass of something warm, here!'

"At this command, half a dozen officious goblins, with a perpetual smile upon their faces, whom Gabriel Grub imagined to be courtiers, on that account, hastily disappeared, and presently returned with a goblet of liquid fire, which they presented to the king.

"'Ah!' cried the goblin, whose cheeks and throat were transparent, as he tossed down the flame, 'this warms one, indeed! Bring a bumper of the same for Mr. Grub.'

"It was in vain for the unfortunate sexton to protest that he was not in the habit of taking anything warm at night; one of the goblins held him while another poured the blazing liquid down his throat; the whole assembly screeched with laughter as he coughed and choked, and wiped away the tears which gushed plentifully from his eyes, after swallowing the burning draught.

"'And now,' said the king, fantastically poking the taper corner of his sugar-loaf hat into the sexton's eyes, and thereby occasioning him the most exquisite pain: 'And now, show the man of misery and gloom, a few of the pictures from our own great storehouse!'

"As the goblin said this, a thick cloud which obscured the remoter end of the cavern, rolled gradually away, and disclosed, apparently at a great distance, a small and scantily furnished, but neat and clean apartment. A crowd of little children were gathered round a bright fire, clinging

to their mother's gown, and gambolling around her chair. The mother occasionally rose, and drew aside the window-curtain, as if to look for some expected object; a frugal meal was ready spread upon the table, and an elbow chair was placed near the fire. A knock was heard at the door; the mother opened it, and the children crowded round her, and clapped their hands for joy, as their father entered. He was wet and weary, and shook the snow from his garments, as the children crowded round him, and seizing his cloak, hat, stick, and gloves, with busy zeal, ran with them from the room. Then, as he sat down to his meal before the fire, the children climbed about his knee, and the mother sat by his side, and all seemed happiness and comfort.

"But a change came upon the view, almost imperceptibly. The scene was altered to a small bed-room, where the fairest and youngest child lay dying; the roses had fled from his cheek, and the light from the eye; and even as the sexton looked upon him with an interest he had never felt or known before, he died. His young brothers and sisters crowded round his little bed, and seized his tiny hand, so cold and heavy; but they shrunk back from its touch, and looked with awe on his infant face; for calm and tranquil as it was and sleeping in rest and peace as the beautiful child seemed to be, they saw that he was dead, and they knew that he was an Angel looking down upon, and blessing them, from a bright and happy Heaven.

"Again the light cloud passed across the picture, and again the subject changed. The father and mother were old and helpless now, and the number of those about them was diminished more than half; but content and cheerfulness sat on every face, and beamed in every eye, as they crowded round the fireside, and told and listened to old stories of earlier and bygone days. Slowly and peacefully, the father sank into the grave, and, soon after, the sharer of all his cares and troubles followed him to a place of rest. The few, who yet survived them, knelt by their tomb, and watered the green turf which covered it, with

their tears; then rose, and turned away: sadly and mournfully, but not with bitter cries, or despairing lamentations, for they knew that they should one day meet again; and once more they mixed with the busy world, and their content and cheerfulness were restored. The cloud settled upon the picture, and concealed it from the sexton's view.

"'What do you think of *that?*' said the goblin, turning his large face towards Gabriel Grub.

"Gabriel murmured out something about its being very pretty, and looked somewhat ashamed, as the goblin bent his fiery eyes upon him.

"'*You* a miserable man!' said the goblin, in a tone of excessive contempt. 'You!' He appeared disposed to add more, but indignation choked his utterance, so he lifted up one of his very pliable legs, and flourishing it above his head a little, to insure his aim, administered a good sound kick to Gabriel Grub; immediately after which, all the goblins in waiting crowded round the wretched sexton, and kicked him without mercy: according to the established and invariable custom of courtiers upon earth, who kick whom royalty kicks, and hug whom royalty hugs.

"'Show him some more!' said the king of the goblins.

"At these words, the cloud was dispelled, and a rich and beautiful landscape was disclosed to view—there is just such another, to this day, within half a mile of the old abbey town. The sun shone from out the clear blue sky, the water sparkled beneath its rays, and the trees looked greener, and the flowers more gay, beneath his cheering influence. The water rippled on, with a pleasant sound; the trees rustled in the light wind that murmured among their leaves; the birds sang upon the boughs; and the lark carolled on high her welcome to the morning. Yes, it was morning; the bright, balmy morning of summer; the minutest leaf, the smallest blade of grass, was instinct with life. The ant crept forth to her daily toil, the butterfly fluttered and basked in the warm rays of the sun; myriads of insects spread their transparent wings, and revelled in their

brief but happy existence. Man walked forth, elated with the scene; and all was brightness and splendour.

"'*You* a miserable man!' said the king of the goblins, in a more contemptuous tone than before. And again the king of the goblins gave his leg a flourish; again it descended on the shoulders of the sexton; and again the attendant goblins imitated the example of their chief.

"Many a time the cloud went and came, and many a lesson it taught to Gabriel Grub, who, although his shoulders smarted with pain from the frequent applications of the goblins' feet, looked on with an interest that nothing could diminish. He saw that men who worked hard, and earned their scanty bread with lives of labour, were cheerful and happy; and that to the most ignorant, the sweet face of nature was a never-failing source of cheerfulness and joy. He saw those who had been delicately nurtured, and tenderly brought up, cheerful under privations, and superior to suffering that would have crushed many of a rougher grain, because they bore within their own bosoms the materials of happiness, contentment, and peace. He saw that women, the tenderest and most fragile of all

God's creatures, were the oftenest superior to sorrow, adversity, and distress; and he saw that it was because they bore, in their own hearts, an inexhaustible well-spring of affection and devotion. Above all, he saw that men like himself, who snarled at the mirth and cheerfulness of others, were the foulest weeds on the fair surface of the earth; and setting all the good of the world against the evil, he came to the conclusion that it was a very decent and respectable sort of world after all. No sooner had he formed it, than the cloud which closed over the last picture, seemed to settle on his senses, and lull him to repose. One by one, the goblins faded from his sight; and as the last one disappeared, he sunk to sleep.

"The day had broken when Gabriel Grub awoke, and found himself lying, at full length on the flat gravestone in the churchyard, with the wicker bottle lying empty by his side, and his coat, spade, and lantern, all well whitened by the last night's frost, scattered on the ground. The stone on which he had first seen the goblin seated stood bolt upright before him, and the grave at which he had worked, the night before, was not far off. At first, he began to doubt the reality of his adventures, but the acute pain in his shoulders when he attempted to rise assured him that the kicking of the goblins was certainly not ideal. He was staggered again by observing no traces of footsteps in the snow on which the goblins had played at leap-frog with the gravestones, but he speedily accounted for this circumstance when he remembered that, being spirits, they would leave no visible impression behind them. So, Gabriel Grub got on his feet as well as he could, for the pain in his back; and brushing the frost off his coat, put it on, and turned his face towards the town.

"But he was an altered man, and he could not bear the thought of returning to a place where his repentance would be scoffed at, and his reformation disbelieved. He hesitated for a few moments; and then turned away to wander where he might, and seek his bread elsewhere.

"The lantern, the spade, and the wicker bottle, were found, that day, in the churchyard. There were a great many speculations about the sexton's fate, at first, but it was speedily determined that he had been carried away by the goblins; and there were not wanting some very credible witnesses who had distinctly seen him whisked through the air on the back of a chestnut horse blind of one eye, with the hind-quarters of a lion, and the tail of a bear. At length all this was devoutly believed; and the new sexton used to exhibit to the curious, for a trifling emolument, a good-sized piece of the church weathercock which had been accidentally kicked off by the aforesaid horse in his aerial flight, and picked up by himself in the churchyard, a year or two afterwards.

"Unfortunately, these stories were somewhat disturbed by the unlooked-for re-appearance of Gabriel Grub himself, some ten years afterwards, a ragged, contented, rheumatic old man. He told his story to the clergyman, and also to the mayor; and in course of time it began to be received, as a matter of history, in which form it has continued down to this very day. The believers in the weathercock tale, having misplaced their confidence once, were not easily prevailed upon to part with it again, so they looked as wise as they could, shrugged their shoulders, touched their foreheads, and murmured something about Gabriel Grub having drunk all the Hollands, and then fallen asleep on the flat tombstone; and they affected to explain what he supposed he had witnessed in the goblin's cavern, by saying that he had seen the world, and grown wiser. But this opinion, which was by no means a popular one at any time, gradually died off; and be the matter how it may, as Gabriel Grub was afflicted with rheumatism to the end of his days, this story has at least one moral, if it teach no better one—and that is, that if a man turn sulky and drink by himself at Christmas time, he may make up his mind to be not a bit the better for it: let the spirits be never so good, or let them be even as many degrees beyond proof, as those which Gabriel Grub saw in the goblin's cavern."

My Christmas Miracle

TAYLOR CALDWELL

For many of us, one Christmas stands out from all the others, the one when the meaning of the day shone clearest.

Although I did not guess it, my own "truest" Christmas began on a rainy spring day in the bleakest year of my life. Recently divorced, I was in my 20s, had no job, and was on my way downtown to go the rounds of the employment offices. I had no umbrella, for my old one had fallen apart, and I could not afford another one. I sat down in the streetcar, and there against the seat was a beautiful silk umbrella with a silver handle inlaid with gold and flecks of bright enamel. I had never seen anything so lovely.

I examined the handle and saw a name engraved among the golden scrolls. The usual procedure would have been to turn in the umbrella to the conductor, but on impulse I decided to take it with me and find the owner myself. I got off the streetcar in a downpour and thankfully opened the umbrella to protect myself. Then I searched a telephone book for the name on the umbrella and found it. I called, and a lady answered.

Yes, she said in surprise, that was her umbrella, which her parents, now dead, had given her for a birthday present. But, she added, it had been stolen from her locker at school (she was a teacher) more than a year before. She was so excited that I forgot I was looking for a job and went directly to her small house. She took the umbrella, and her eyes filled with tears.

The teacher wanted to give me a reward, but—though $20 was all I had in the world—her happiness at retrieving this special possession was such that to have accepted money would have spoiled something. We talked for a while, and I must have given her my address. I don't remember.

The next six months were wretched. I was able to obtain only temporary employment here and there, for a small salary, though this was what they now call the Roaring Twenties. But I put aside 25 or 50 cents when I could afford it for my little girl's Christmas presents. (It took me six months to save $8.) My last job ended the day before Christmas, my $30 rent was soon due, and I had $15 to my name—which Peggy and I would need for food. She was home from her convent boarding school and was excitedly looking forward to her gifts the next day, which I had already purchased. I had bought her a small tree, and we were going to decorate it that night.

The stormy air was full of the sound of Christmas merriment as I walked from the streetcar to my small apartment. Bells rang and children shouted in the bitter dusk of the evening, and windows were lighted and everyone was running and laughing. But there would be no Christmas for me, I knew, no gifts, no remembrance whatsoever. As I struggled through the snowdrifts, I just about reached the lowest point in my life. Unless a miracle happened I would be homeless in January, foodless, jobless. I had prayed steadily for weeks, and there had been no answer but this coldness and darkness, this harsh air, this abandonment. God and men had completely forgotten me. I felt old as death, and as lonely. What was to become of us?

I looked in my mailbox. There were only bills in it, a sheaf of them, and two white envelopes which I was sure contained more bills. I went up three dusty flights of stairs, and I cried, shivering in my thin coat. But I made myself smile so I

could greet my little daughter with a pretense of happiness. She opened the door for me and threw herself in my arms, screaming joyously and demanding that we decorate the tree immediately.

Peggy was not yet six years old, and had been alone all day while I worked. She had set our kitchen table for our evening meal, proudly, and put pans out and the three cans of food which would be our dinner. For some reason, when I looked at those pans and cans, I felt brokenhearted. We would have only hamburgers for our Christmas dinner tomorrow, and gelatin. I stood in the cold little kitchen, and misery overwhelmed me. For the first time in my life, I doubted the existence of God and His mercy, and the coldness in my heart was colder than ice.

The doorbell rang, and Peggy ran fleetly to answer it, calling that it must be Santa Claus. Then I heard a man talking heartily to her and went to the door. He was a delivery man, and his arms were full of big parcels, and he was laughing at my child's frenzied joy and her dancing. "This is a mistake," I said, but he read the name on the parcels, and they were for me. When he had gone I could only stare at the boxes. Peggy and I sat on the floor and opened them. A huge doll, three times the size of the one I had bought for her. Gloves. Candy. A beautiful leather purse. Incredible! I looked for the name of the sender. It was the teacher, the address simply "California," where she had moved.

Our dinner that night was the most delicious I had ever eaten. I could only pray in myself, "Thank You, Father." I forgot I had no money for the rent and only $15 in my purse and no job. My child and I ate and laughed together in happiness. Then we decorated the little tree and marveled at it. I put Peggy to bed and set up her gifts around the tree, and a sweet peace flooded me like a benediction. I had some hope again. I could even examine the sheaf of bills without cringing. Then I opened the two white envelopes. One contained a check for $30 from a company I had worked for briefly in the summer. It was, said a note, my "Christmas bonus." My rent!

The other envelope was an offer of a permanent position with the government—to begin two days after Christmas. I sat with the letter in my hand and the check on the table before me, and I think that was the most joyful moment of my life up to that time.

The church bells began to ring. I hurriedly looked at my child, who was sleeping blissfully, and ran down to the street. Everywhere people were walking to church to celebrate the birth of the Saviour. People smiled at me and I smiled back. The storm had stopped, the sky was pure and glittering with stars.

"The Lord is born!" sang the bells to the crystal night and the laughing darkness. Someone began to sing, "Come, all ye faithful!" I joined in and sang with the strangers all about me.

I am not alone at all, I thought. *I was never alone at all.*

And that, of course, is the message of Christmas. We are never alone. Not when the night is darkest, the wind coldest, the world seemingly most indifferent. For this is still the time God chooses.

The Legend of the Christmas Rose

SELMA LAGERLÖF

Robber Mother, who lived in Robbers' Cave up in Göinge forest, went down to the village one day on a begging tour. Robber Father, who was an outlawed man, did not dare to leave the forest. She took with her five youngsters, and each youngster bore a sack on his back as long as himself. When Robber Mother stepped inside the door of a cabin, no one dared refuse to give her whatever she demanded; for she was not above coming back the following night and setting fire to the house if she had not been well received. Robber Mother and her brood were worse than a pack of wolves, and many a man felt like running a spear through them; but it was never done, because they all knew that the man stayed up in the forest, and he would have known how to wreak vengeance if anything had happened to the children or the old woman.

Now that Robber Mother went from house to house and begged, she came to Övid, which at that time was a cloister. She rang the bell of the cloister gate and asked for food. The watchman let down a small wicket in the gate and handed her six round bread cakes—one for herself and one for each of the five children.

While the mother was standing quietly at the gate, her youngsters were running about. And now one of them came and pulled at her skirt, as a signal that he had discovered something which she ought to come and see, and Robber Mother followed him promptly.

The entire cloister was surrounded by a high and strong wall, but the youngster had managed to find a little back gate which stood ajar. When Robber Mother got there, she pushed the gate open and walked inside without asking leave, as it was her custom to do.

Övid Cloister was managed at that time by Abbot Hans, who knew all about herbs. Just within the cloister wall he had planted a little herb garden, and it was into this that the old woman had forced her way.

At first glance Robber Mother was so astonished that she paused at the gate. It was high summertide, and Abbot Hans' garden was so full of flowers that the eyes were fairly dazzled by the blues, reds, and yellows, as one looked into it. But presently an indulgent smile spread over her features, and she started to walk up a narrow path that lay between many flower beds.

In the garden a lay brother walked about, pulling up weeds. It was he who had left the door in the wall open, that he might throw the weeds and tares on the rubbish heap outside.

When he saw Robber Mother coming in, with all five youngsters in tow, he ran toward her at once and ordered them away. But the beggar woman walked right on as before. The lay brother knew of no other remedy than to run into the cloister and call for help.

He returned with two stalwart monks, and Robber Mother saw that now it meant business! She let out a perfect volley of shrieks, and, throwing herself upon the monks, clawed and bit at them; so did all the youngsters. The men soon learned that she could overpower them, and all they could do was go back into the cloister for reinforcements.

As they ran through the passage-way which led to the cloister, they met Abbot Hans, who came rushing out to learn what all this noise was about.

He upbraided them for using force and forbade their calling for help. He sent both monks back to their work, and although he was an old and fragile man, he took with him only the lay brother.

He came up to the woman and asked in a mild tone if the garden pleased her.

Robber Mother turned defiantly toward Abbot Hans, for she expected only to be trapped and overpowered. But when she noticed his white hair and bent form, she answered peaceably, "First, when I saw this, I thought I had never seen a prettier garden; but now I see that it can't be compared with one I know of. If you could see the garden of which I am thinking you would uproot all the flowers planted here and cast them away like weeds."

The Abbot's assistant was hardly less proud of the flowers than the Abbot himself, and after hearing her remarks he laughed derisively.

Robber Mother grew crimson with rage to think that her word was doubted, and she cried out: "You monks, who are holy men, certainly must know that on every Christmas Eve the great Göinge forest is transformed into a beautiful garden, to commemorate the hour of our Lord's birth. We who live in the forest have seen this happen every year. And in that garden I have seen flowers so lovely that I dared not lift my hand to pluck them."

Ever since his childhood, Abbot Hans had heard it said that on every Christmas Eve the forest was dressed in holiday glory. He had often longed to see it, but he had never had the good fortune. Eagerly he begged and implored Robber Mother that he might come up to the Robbers' Cave on Christmas Eve. If she would only send one of her children to show him the way, he could ride up there alone, and he would never betray them—on the contrary, he would reward them insofar as it lay in his power.

Robber Mother said no at first, for she was thinking of Robber Father and of the peril which might befall him should she permit Abbot Hans to ride up to their cave. At the same time the desire to prove to the monk that the garden which she knew was more beautiful than his got the better of her, and she gave in.

"But more than one follower you cannot take with you," said she, "and you are not to waylay us or trap us, as sure as you are a holy man."

This Abbot Hans promised, and then Robber Mother went her way.

It happened that Archbishop Absalon from Lund came to Övid and remained through the night. The lay brother heard Abbot Hans telling the Bishop about Robber Father and asking him for a letter of ransom for the man, that he might lead an honest life among respectable folk.

But the Archbishop replied that he did not care to let the robber loose among honest folk in the villages. It would be best for all that he remain in the forest.

Then Abbot Hans grew zealous and told the Bishop all about Göinge forest, which, every year at Yuletide, clothed itself in summer bloom around the Robbers' Cave. "If these bandits are not so bad but that God's glories can be made manifest to them, surely we cannot be too wicked to experience the same blessing."

The Archbishop knew how to answer Abbot Hans. "This much I will promise you, Abbot Hans," he said, smiling, "that any day you send me a blossom from the garden in Göinge forest, I will give you letters of ransom for all the outlaws you may choose to plead for."

The following Christmas Eve Abbot Hans was on his way to the forest. One of Robber Mother's wild youngsters ran ahead of him, and close behind him was the lay brother.

It turned out to be a long and hazardous ride. They climbed steep and slippery side paths, crawled over swamp and marsh, and pushed through windfall and bramble. Just as daylight was waning, the robber boy guided them across a forest meadow, skirted by tall, naked leaf trees and green fir trees. Back of the meadow loomed a mountain wall, and in this wall they saw a door of thick boards. Now Abbot Hans understood that they had arrived, and dismounted. The child

opened the heavy door for him, and he looked
into a poor mountain grotto, with bare stone
walls. Robber Mother was seated before a log fire
that burned in the middle of the floor. Alongside
the walls were beds of virgin pine and moss, and
on one of these beds lay Robber Father asleep.

"Come in, you out there!" shouted Robber
Mother without rising, "and fetch the horses in
with you, so they won't be destroyed by the night
cold."

Abbot Hans walked boldly into the cave, and
the lay brother followed. Here were wretchedness

and poverty! and nothing was done to celebrate
Christmas.

Robber Mother spoke in a tone as haughty and
dictatorial as any well-to-do peasant woman. "Sit
down by the fire and warm yourself, Abbot
Hans," said she; "and if you have food with you,
eat, for the food which we in the forest prepare
you wouldn't care to taste. And if you are tired
after the long journey, you can lie down on one of
these beds to sleep. You needn't be afraid of
oversleeping, for I'm sitting here by the fire keeping watch. I shall awaken you in time to see that

which you have come up here to see."

Abbot Hans obeyed Robber Mother and brought forth his food sack; but he was so fatigued after the journey he was hardly able to eat, and as soon as he could stretch himself on the bed, he fell asleep.

The lay brother was also assigned a bed to rest and he dropped into a doze.

When he woke up, he saw that Abbot Hans had left his bed and was sitting by the fire talking with Robber Mother. The outlawed robber sat also by the fire. He was a tall, raw-boned man with a dull, sluggish appearance. His back was turned to Abbot Hans, as though he would have it appear that he was not listening to the conversation.

Abbot Hans was telling Robber Mother all about the Christmas preparations he had seen on the journey, reminding her of Christmas feasts and games which she must have known in her youth, when she lived at peace with mankind.

At first Robber Mother answered in short, gruff sentences, but by degrees she became more

subdued and listened more intently. Suddenly Robber Father turned toward Abbot Hans and shook his clenched fist in his face. "You miserable monk! did you come here to coax from me my wife and children? Don't you know that I am an outlaw and may not leave the forest?"

Abbot Hans looked him fearlessly in the eyes. "It is my purpose to get a letter of ransom for you from Archbishop Absalon," said he. He had hardly finished speaking when the robber and his wife burst out laughing. They knew well enough the kind of mercy a forest robber could expect from Bishop Absalon!

"Oh, if I get a letter of ransom from Absalon," said Robber Father, "then I'll promise you that never again will I steal so much as a goose."

Suddenly Robber Mother rose. "You sit here and talk, Abbot Hans," she said, "so that we are forgetting to look at the forest. Now I can hear, even in this cave, how the Christmas bells are ringing."

The words were barely uttered when they all sprang up and rushed out. But in the forest it was still dark night and bleak winter. The only thing they marked was a distant clang borne on a light south wind.

When the bells had been ringing a few moments, a sudden illumination penetrated the forest; the next moment it was dark again, and then light came back. It pushed its way forward between the stark trees, like a shimmering mist. The darkness merged into a faint daybreak. Then Abbot Hans saw that the snow had vanished from the ground, as if someone had removed a carpet, and the earth began to take on a green covering. The moss-tufts thickened and raised themselves, and the spring blossoms shot upward their swelling buds, which already had a touch of color.

Again it grew hazy; but almost immediately there came a new wave of light. Then the leaves of the trees burst into bloom, crossbeaks hopped from branch to branch, and the woodpeckers hammered on the limbs until the splinters fairly flew around them. A flock of starlings from up country lighted in a fir top to rest.

When the next warm wind came along, the blueberries ripened and the baby squirrels began playing on the branches of the trees.

The next light wave that came rushing in brought with it the scent of newly ploughed acres. Pine and spruce trees were so thickly clothed with red cones that they shone like crimson mantles and forest flowers covered the ground till it was all red, blue, and yellow.

Abbot Hans bent down to the earth and broke off a wild strawberry blossom, and, as he straightened up, the berry ripened in his hand.

The mother fox came out of her lair with a big litter of black-legged young. She went up to Robber Mother and scratched at her skirt, and Robber Mother bent down to her and praised her young.

Robber Mother's youngsters let out perfect shrieks of delight. They stuffed themselves with wild strawberries that hung on the bushes. One of them played with a litter of young hares; another ran a race with some young crows, which had hopped from their nest before they were really ready.

Robber Father was standing out on a marsh eating raspberries. When he glanced up, a big black bear stood beside him. Robber Father broke off a twig and struck the bear on the nose. "Keep to your own ground, you!" he said; "this is my turf." The huge bear turned around and lumbered off in another direction.

Then all the flowers whose seeds had been brought from foreign lands began to blossom. The loveliest roses climbed up the mountain wall in a race with the blackberry vines, and from the forest meadow sprang flowers as large as human faces.

Abbot Hans thought of the flower he was to pluck for Bishop Absalon; but each new flower that appeared was more beautiful than the others, and he wanted to choose the most beautiful of all.

Then Abbot Hans marked how all grew still; the birds hushed their songs, the flowers ceased growing, and the young foxes played no more. From far in the distance faint harp tones were heard, and celestial song, like a soft murmur, reached him.

He clasped his hands and dropped to his knees. His face was radiant with bliss.

But beside Abbot Hans stood the lay brother who had accompanied him. In his mind there were dark thoughts. "This cannot be a true miracle," he thought, "since it is revealed to malefactors. This does not come from God, but is sent hither by Satan. It is the Evil One's power that is tempting us and compelling us to see that which has no real existence."

The angel throng was so near now that Abbot Hans saw their bright forms through the forest branches. The lay brother saw them, too; but back of all this wondrous beauty he saw only some dread evil.

All the while the birds had been circling around the head of Abbot Hans, and they let him take them in his hands. But all the animals were afraid of the lay brother; no bird perched on his shoulder, no snake played at his feet. Then there came a little forest dove. When she marked that the angels were nearing, she plucked up courage and flew down on the lay brother's shoulder and laid her head against his cheek.

Then it appeared to him as if sorcery were come right upon him, to tempt and corrupt him. He struck with his hand at the forest dove and cried in such a loud voice that it rang throughout the forest, "Go thou back to hell, whence thou art come!"

Just then the angels were so near that Abbot Hans felt the feathery touch of their great wings, and he bowed down to earth in reverent greeting.

But when the lay brother's words sounded, their song was hushed and the holy guests turned in flight. At the same time the light and the mild warmth vanished in unspeakable terror for the darkness and cold in a human heart. Darkness sank over the earth, like a coverlet; frost came, all the growths shrivelled up; the animals and birds hastened away; the leaves dropped from the trees, rustling like rain.

Abbot Hans felt how his heart, which had but

lately swelled with bliss, was now contracting with insufferable agony. "I can never outlive this," thought he, "that the angels from heaven had been so close to me and were driven away; that they wanted to sing Christmas carols for me and were driven to flight."

Then he remembered the flower he had promised Bishop Absalon, and at the last moment he fumbled among the leaves and moss to try and find a blossom. But he sensed how the ground under his fingers froze and how the white snow came gliding over the ground. Then his heart caused him even greater anguish. He could not rise, but fell prostrate on the ground and lay there.

When the robber folk and the lay brother had groped their way back to the cave, they missed Abbot Hans. They took brands with them and went out to search for him. They found him dead upon the coverlet of snow.

When Abbot Hans had been carried down to Övid, those who took charge of the dead saw that he held his right hand locked tight around something which he must have grasped at the moment of death. When they finally got his hand open, they found that the thing which he had held in such an iron grip was a pair of white root bulbs, which he had torn from among the moss and leaves.

When the lay brother who had accompanied Abbot Hans saw the bulbs, he took them and planted them in Abbot Hans' herb garden.

He guarded them the whole year to see if any flower would spring from them. But in vain he waited through the spring, the summer, and the autumn. Finally, when winter had set in and all the leaves and the flowers were dead, he ceased caring for them.

But when Christmas Eve came again, he was so strongly reminded of Abbot Hans that he wandered out into the garden to think of him. And look! as he came to the spot where he had planted the bare root bulbs, he saw that from them had sprung flourishing green stalks, which bore beautiful flowers with silver white leaves.

He called out all the monks at Övid, and when they saw that this plant bloomed on Christmas Eve, when all the other growths were as if dead, they understood that this flower had in truth been plucked by Abbot Hans from the Christmas garden in Göinge forest. Then the lay brother asked the monks if he might take a few blossoms to Bishop Absalon.

When Bishop Absalon beheld the flowers, which had sprung from the earth in darkest winter, he turned as pale as if he had met a ghost. He sat in silence a moment; thereupon he said, "Abbot Hans has faithfully kept his word and I shall also keep mine."

He handed the letter of ransom to the lay brother, who departed at once for the Robbers' Cave. When he stepped in there on Christmas Day, the robber came toward him with axe uplifted. "I'd like to hack you monks into bits, as many as you are!" said he. "It must be your fault that Göinge forest did not last night dress itself in Christmas bloom."

"The fault is mine alone," said the lay brother, "and I will gladly die for it; but first I must deliver a message from Abbot Hans." And he drew forth the Bishop's letter and told the man that he was free.

Robber Father stood there pale and speechless, but Robber Mother said in his name, "Abbot Hans has indeed kept his word, and Robber Father will keep his."

When the robber and his wife left the cave, the lay brother moved in and lived all alone in the forest, in constant meditation and prayer that his hard-heartedness might be forgiven him.

But Göinge forest never again celebrated the hour of our Savior's birth; and of all its glory, there lives today only the plant which Abbot Hans had plucked. It has been named CHRISTMAS ROSE. And each year at Christmastide she sends forth from the earth her green stalks and white blossoms, as if she never could forget that she had once grown in the great Christmas garden at Göinge forest.

A Christmas Dream, and How It Came True

LOUISA MAY ALCOTT

"I'm so tired of Christmas I wish there never would be another one!" exclaimed a discontented-looking little girl, as she sat idly watching her mother arrange a pile of gifts two days before they were to be given.

"Why, Effie, what a dreadful thing to say! You are as bad as old Scrooge; and I'm afraid something will happen to you, as it did to him, if you don't care for dear Christmas," answered mamma, almost dropping the silver horn she was filling with delicious candies.

"Who was Scrooge? What happened to him?" asked Effie, with a glimmer of interest in her listless face, as she picked out the sourest lemon-drop she could find; for nothing sweet suited her just then.

"He was one of Dickens's best people, and you can read the charming story some day. He hated Christmas until a strange dream showed him how dear and beautiful it was, and made a better man of him."

"I shall read it; for I like dreams, and have a great many curious ones myself. But they don't keep me from being tired of Christmas," said Effie, poking discontentedly among the sweeties for something worth eating.

"Why are you tired of what should be the happiest time of all the year?" asked mamma, anxiously.

"Perhaps I shouldn't be if I had something new. But it is always the same, and there isn't any more surprise about it. I always find heaps of goodies in my stocking. Don't like some of them, and soon get tired of those I do like. We always have a great dinner, and I eat too much, and feel ill next day. Then there is a Christmas tree somewhere, with a doll on top, or a stupid old Santa Claus, and children dancing and scream-ing over bonbons and toys that break, and shiny things that are of no use. Really, mamma, I've had so many Christmases all alike that I don't think I *can* bear another one." And Effie laid herself flat on the sofa, as if the mere idea was too much for her.

Her mother laughed at her despair, but was sorry to see her little girl so discontented, when she had everything to make her happy, and had known but ten Christmas days.

"Suppose we don't give you *any* presents at all,—how would that suit you?" asked mamma, anxious to please her spoiled child.

"I should like one large and splendid one, and one dear little one, to remember some very nice person by," said Effie, who was a fanciful little body, full of odd whims and notions, which her friends loved to gratify, regardless of time, trouble, or money; for she was the last of three little girls, and very dear to all the family.

"Well, my darling, I will see what I can do to please you, and not say a word until all is ready. If I could only get a new idea to start with!" And mamma went on tying up her pretty bundles with a thoughtful face, while Effie strolled to the window to watch the rain that kept her indoors and made her dismal.

"Seems to me poor children have better times than rich ones. I can't go out, and there is a girl about my age splashing along, without any maid to fuss about rubbers and cloaks and umbrellas and colds. I wish I was a beggar-girl."

"Would you like to be hungry, cold, and ragged, to beg all day, and sleep on an ash-heap at night?" asked mamma, wondering what would come next.

"Cinderella did, and had a nice time in the end. This girl out here has a basket of scraps on

her arm, and a big old shawl all round her, and doesn't seem to care a bit, though the water runs out of the toes of her boots. She goes paddling along, laughing at the rain, and eating a cold potato as if it tasted nicer than the chicken and ice-cream I had for dinner. Yes, I do think poor children are happier than rich ones."

"So do I, sometimes. At the Orphan Asylum to-day I saw two dozen merry little souls who have no parents, no home, and no hope of Christmas beyond a stick of candy or a cake. I wish you had been there to see how happy they were, playing with the old toys some richer children had sent them."

"You may give them all mine; I'm so tired of them I never want to see them again," said Effie, turning from the window to the pretty baby-house full of everything a child's heart could desire.

"I will, and let you begin again with something that you will not tire of, if I can only find it." And mamma knit her brows trying to discover some grand surprise for this child who didn't care for Christmas.

Nothing more was said then; and, wandering off to the library, Effie found "A Christmas Carol," and, curling herself up in the sofa corner, read it all before tea. Some of it she did not understand; but she laughed and cried over many parts of the charming story, and felt better without knowing why.

All the evening she thought of poor Tiny Tim, Mrs. Cratchit with the pudding, and the stout old gentleman who danced so gayly that "his legs twinkled in the air." Presently bedtime arrived.

"Come, now, and toast your feet," said Effie's nurse, "while I do your pretty hair and tell stories."

"I'll have a fairy tale to-night, a very interesting one," commanded Effie, as she put on her blue silk wrapper and little fur-lined slippers to sit before the fire and have her long curls brushed.

So Nursey told her best tales; and when at last the child lay down under her lace curtains, her head was full of a curious jumble of Christmas elves, poor children, snow-storms, sugar-plums and surprises. So it is no wonder that she dreamed all night, and this was the dream, which she never quite forgot.

She found herself sitting on a stone, in the middle of a great field, all alone. The snow was falling fast, a bitter wind whistled by, and night was coming on. She felt hungry, cold, and tired, and did not know where to go nor what to do.

"I wanted to be a beggar-girl, and now I am one; but I don't like it, and wish somebody would come and take care of me. I don't know who I am, and I think I must be lost," thought Effie, with the curious interest one takes in one's self in dreams.

But the more she thought about it, the more bewildered she felt. Faster fell the snow, colder blew the wind, darker grew the night; and poor Effie made up her mind that she was quite forgotten and left to freeze alone. The tears were chilled on her cheeks, her feet felt like icicles, and her heart died within her, so hungry, frightened, and forlorn was she. Laying her head on her knees, she gave herself up for lost, and sat there with the great flakes fast turning her to a little white mound, when suddenly the sound of music reached her, and starting up, she looked and listened with all her eyes and ears.

Far away a dim light shone, and a voice was heard singing. She tried to run toward the welcome glimmer, but could not stir, and stood like a small statue of expectation while the light drew nearer, and the sweet words of the song grew clearer.

From our happy home
Through the world we roam
One week in all the year,
Making winter spring
With the joy we bring
For Christmas-tide is here.

Now the eastern star
Shines from afar
To light the poorest home;

Hearts warmer grow,
Gifts freely flow,
For Christmas-tide has come.

Now gay trees rise
Before young eyes,
Abloom with tempting cheer;
Blithe voices sing,
And blithe bells ring,
For Christmas-tide is here.

Oh, happy chime,
Oh, blessed time,
That draws us all so near!
"Welcome, dear day,"
All creatures say,
For Christmas-tide is here.

A child's voice sang, a child's hand carried the little candle and in the circle of soft light it shed, Effie saw a pretty child coming to her through the night and snow. A rosy, smiling creature, wrapped in white fur, with a wreath of green and scarlet holly on its shining hair, the magic candle in one hand and the other outstretched as if to shower gifts and warmly press all other hands.

Effie forgot to speak as this bright vision came nearer, leaving no trace of footsteps in the snow, only lighting the way with its little candle, and filling the air with the music of its song.

"Dear child, you are lost, and I have come to find you," said the stranger, taking Effie's cold hands in his, with a smile like sunshine, while every holly berry glowed like a little fire.

"Do you know me?" asked Effie, feeling no fear, but a great gladness, at his coming.

"I know all children, and go to find them; for this is my holiday, and I gather them from all parts of the world to be merry with me once a year."

"Are you an angel?" asked Effie, looking for the wings.

"No; I am a Christmas spirit, and live with my mates in a pleasant place, getting ready for our holiday, when we are let out to roam about the world, helping make this a happy time for all who

will let us in. Will you come and see how we work?"

"I will go anywhere with you. Don't leave me again," cried Effie, gladly.

"First I will make you comfortable. That is what we love to do. You are cold, and you shall be warm; hungry, and I will feed you; sorrowful, and I will make you gay."

With a wave of his candle all three miracles were wrought,—for the snow-flakes turned to a white fur cloak and hood on Effie's head and shoulders; a bowl of hot soup came sailing to her lips, and vanished when she had eagerly drunk the last drop; and suddenly the dismal field changed to a new world so full of wonders that all her troubles were forgotten in a minute.

Bells were ringing so merrily that it was hard to keep from dancing. Green garlands hung on the walls, and every tree was a Christmas tree full of toys, and blazing with candles that never went out.

In one place many little spirits sewed like mad on warm clothes, turning off work faster than any sewing-machine ever invented, and great piles were made ready to be sent to poor people. Other busy creatures packed money into purses, and wrote checks which they sent flying away on the wind,—a lovely kind of snow-storm to fall into a world below full of poverty.

Older and graver spirits were looking over piles of little books, in which the records of the past year were kept, telling how different people had spent it, and what sort of gifts they deserved. Some got peace, some disappointment, some remorse and sorrow, some great joy and hope. The rich had generous thoughts sent them; the poor, gratitude and contentment. Children had more love and duty to parents; and parents renewed patience, wisdom, and satisfaction for and in their children. No one was forgotten.

"Please tell me what splendid place this is," asked Effie, as soon as she could collect her wits after the first look at all these astonishing things.

"This is the Christmas world; and here we work all the year round, never tired of getting

ready for the happy day. See, these are the saints just setting off; for some have far to go, and the children must not be disappointed."

As he spoke the spirit pointed to four gates, out of which four great sleighs were just driving, laden with toys, while a jolly old Santa Claus sat in the middle of each, drawing on his mittens and tucking up his wraps for a long cold drive.

"Why, I thought there was only one Santa Claus, and even he was a humbug," cried Effie, astonished at the sight.

"Never give up your faith in the sweet old stories, even after you come to see that they are only the pleasant shadow of a lovely truth."

Just then the sleighs went off with a great jingling of bells and pattering of reindeer hoofs, while all the spirits gave a cheer that was heard in the lower world, where people said, "Hear the stars sing."

"I never will say there isn't any Santa Claus again. Now, show me more."

"You will like to see this place, I think, and may learn something here perhaps."

The spirit smiled as he led the way to a little door, through which Effie peeped into a world of dolls. Baby-houses were in full blast, with dolls of all sorts going on like live people. Waxen ladies sat in their parlors elegantly dressed; black dolls cooked in the kitchens; nurses walked out with the bits of dollies; and the streets were full of tin soldiers marching, wooden horses prancing, express wagons rumbling, and little men hurrying to and fro. Shops were there, and tiny people buying legs of mutton, pounds of tea, mites of clothes, and everything dolls use or wear or want.

But presently she saw that in some ways the dolls improved upon the manners and customs of human beings, and she watched eagerly to learn why they did these things. A fine Paris doll driving in her carriage took up a black worsted Dinah who was hobbling along with a basket of clean clothes, and carried her to her journey's end, as if it were the proper thing to do. Another interesting china lady took off her comfortable red cloak and put it round a poor wooden creature done up

in a paper shift, and so badly painted that its face would have sent some babies into fits.

"Seems to me I once knew a rich girl who didn't give her things to poor girls. I wish I could remember who she was, and tell her to be as kind as that china doll," said Effie, much touched at the sweet way the pretty creature wrapped up the poor fright, and then ran off in her little gray gown to buy a shiny fowl stuck on a wooden platter for her invalid mother's dinner.

"We recall these things to people's minds by dreams. I think the girl you speak of won't forget this one." And the spirit smiled, as if he enjoyed some joke which she did not see.

A little bell rang as she looked, and away scampered the children into the red-and-green school-house with the roof that lifted up, so one could see how nicely they sat at their desks with mites of books, or drew on the inch-square blackboards with crumbs of chalk.

"They know their lessons very well, and are as still as mice. We make a great racket at our school, and get bad marks every day. I shall tell the girls they had better mind what they do, or their dolls will be better scholars than they are," said Effie, much impressed, as she peeped in and saw no rod in the hand of the little mistress, who looked up and shook her head at the intruder, as if begging her to go away before the order of the school was disturbed.

Effie retired at once, but could not resist one

look in at the window of a fine mansion, where the family were at dinner, the children behaved so well at table, and never grumbled a bit when their mamma said they could not have any more fruit.

"Now, show me something else," she said, as they came again to the low door that led out of Doll-land.

"You have seen how we prepare for Christmas; let me show you where we love best to send our good and happy gifts," answered the spirit, giving her his hand again.

"I know. I've seen ever so many," began Effie, thinking of her own Christmases.

"No, you have never seen what I will show you. Come away, and remember what you see to-night."

Like a flash that bright world vanished, and Effie found herself in a part of the city she had never seen before. It was far away from the gayer places, where every store was brilliant with lights and full of pretty things, and every house wore a festival air, while people hurried to and fro with merry greetings. It was down among the dingy streets where the poor lived, and where there was no making ready for Christmas.

Hungry women looked in at the shabby shops, longing to buy meat and bread, but empty pockets forbade. Tipsy men drank up their wages in the bar-rooms; and in many cold dark chambers little children huddled under the thin blankets, trying to forget their misery in sleep.

No nice dinners filled the air with savory smells, no gay trees dropped toys and bonbons into eager hands, no little stockings hung in rows beside the chimney-piece ready to be filled, no happy sounds of music, gay voices, and dancing feet were heard; and there were no signs of Christmas anywhere.

"Don't they have any in this place?" asked Effie, shivering, as she held fast the spirit's hand, following where he led her.

"We come to bring it. Let me show you our best workers." And the spirit pointed to some sweet-faced men and women who came stealing into the poor houses, working such beautiful miracles that Effie could only stand and watch.

Some slipped money into the empty pockets, and sent the happy mothers to buy all the comforts they needed; others led the drunken men out of temptation, and took them home to find safer pleasures there. Fires were kindled on cold hearths, tables spread as if by magic, and warm clothes wrapped round shivering limbs. Flowers suddenly bloomed in the chambers of the sick; old people found themselves remembered; sad hearts were consoled by a tender word, and wicked ones softened by the story of Him who forgave all sin.

But the sweetest work was for the children; and Effie held her breath to watch these human fairies hang up and fill the little stockings without which a child's Christmas is not perfect, putting in things that once she would have thought very humble presents, but which now seemed beautiful and precious because these poor babies had nothing.

"That is so beautiful! I wish I could make merry Christmases as these good people do, and be loved and thanked as they are," said Effie, softly, as she watched the busy men and women do their work and steal away without thinking of any reward but their own satisfaction.

"You can if you will. I have shown you the way. Try it, and see how happy your own holiday will be hereafter."

As he spoke, the spirit seemed to put his arms about her, and vanished with a kiss.

"Oh, stay and show me more!" cried Effie, trying to hold him fast.

"Darling, wake up, and tell me why you are smiling in your sleep," said a voice in her ear; and, opening her eyes, there was mamma bending over her, and morning sunshine streaming into the room.

"Are they all gone? Did you hear the bells? Wasn't it splendid?" she asked, rubbing her eyes, and looking about her for the pretty child who was so real and sweet.

"You have been dreaming at a great rate,— talking in your sleep, laughing, and clapping your hands as if you were cheering some one. Tell me what was so splendid," said mamma, smoothing the tumbled hair and lifting up the sleepy head.

Then, while she was being dressed, Effie told her dream, and Nursey thought it very wonderful; but mamma smiled to see how curiously things the child had thought, read, heard, and seen through the day were mixed up in her sleep.

"The spirit said I could work lovely miracles if I tried; but I don't know how to begin, for I have no magic candle to make feasts appear, and light up groves of Christmas trees, as he did," said Effie, sorrowfully.

"Yes, you have. We will do it! we will do it!" And clapping her hands, mamma suddenly began to dance all over the room as if she had lost her wits.

"How? how? You must tell me, mamma," cried

Effie, dancing after her, and ready to believe anything possible when she remembered the adventures of the past night.

"I've got it! I've got it!—the new idea. A splendid one, if I can only carry it out!" And mamma waltzed the little girl round till her curls flew wildly in the air, while Nursey laughed as if she would die.

"Tell me! tell me!" shrieked Effie.

"No, no; it is a surprise,—a grand surprise for Christmas day!" sung mamma, evidently charmed with her happy thought. "Now, come to breakfast; for we must work like bees if we want to play spirits to-morrow. You and Nursey will go out shopping, and get heaps of things, while I arrange matters behind the scenes."

They were running downstairs as mamma spoke, and Effie called out breathlessly,—

"It won't be a surprise; for I know you are going to ask some poor children here, and have a tree or something. It won't be like my dream; for they had ever so many trees, and more children than we can find anywhere."

"There will be no tree, no party, no dinner, in this house at all, and no presents for you. Won't that be a surprise?" And mamma laughed at Effie's bewildered face.

"Do it. I shall like it, I think; and I won't ask any questions, so it will all burst upon me when the time comes," she said; and she ate her breakfast thoughtfully, for this really would be a new sort of Christmas.

All that morning Effie trotted after Nursey in and out of shops, buying dozens of barking dogs, woolly lambs and squeaking birds; tiny tea-sets, gay picture-books, mittens and hoods, dolls and candy. Parcel after parcel was sent home; but when Effie returned she saw no trace of them, though she peeped everywhere. Nursey chuckled, but wouldn't give a hint, and went out again in the afternoon with a long list of more things to buy; while Effie wandered forlornly about the house, missing the usual merry stir that went before the Christmas dinner and the evening fun.

As for mamma, she was quite invisible all day, and came in at night so tired that she could only lie on the sofa to rest, smiling as if some very pleasant thought made her happy in spite of weariness.

"Is the surprise going on all right?" asked Effie, anxiously; for it seemed an immense time to wait till another evening came.

"Beautifully! better than I expected; for several of my good friends are helping, or I couldn't have done it as I wish. I know you will like it, dear, and long remember this new way of making Christmas merry."

Mamma gave her a very tender kiss, and Effie went to bed.

The next day was a very strange one; for when she woke there was no stocking to examine, no pile of gifts under her napkin, no one said "Merry Christmas!" to her, and the dinner was just as usual to her. Mamma vanished again, and Nursey kept wiping her eyes and saying: "The dear things! It's the prettiest idea I ever heard of. No one but your blessed ma could have done it."

"Do stop, Nursey, or I shall go crazy because I don't know the secret!" cried Effie, more than once; and she kept her eye on the clock, for at seven in the evening the surprise was to come off.

The longed-for hour arrived at last, and the child was too excited to ask questions when Nurse put on her cloak and hood, led her to the carriage, and they drove away, leaving their house the one dark and silent one in the row.

"I feel like the girls in the fairy tales who are led off to strange places and see fine things," said Effie, in a whisper, as they jingled through the gay streets.

"Ah, my deary, it is like a fairy tale, I do assure you, and you will see finer things than most children will to-night. Steady, now, and do just as I tell you, and don't say one word, whatever you see," answered Nursey, quite quivering with excitement as she patted a large box in her lap, and nodded and laughed with twinkling eyes.

They drove into a dark yard, and Effie was led through a back door to a little room, where Nurse coolly proceeded to take off not only her cloak and hood, but her dress and shoes also. Effie

stared and bit her lips, but kept still until out of the box came a little white fur coat and boots, a wreath of holly leaves and berries, and a candle with a frill of gold paper round it. A long "Oh!" escaped her then; and when she was dressed and saw herself in the glass, she started back, exclaiming, "Why, Nursey, I look like the spirit in my dream!"

"So you do; and that's the part you are to play, my pretty! Now whist, while I blind your eyes and put you in your place."

"Shall I be afraid?" whispered Effie, full of wonder; for as they went out she heard the sound of many voices, the tramp of many feet, and in spite of the bandage, was sure a great light shone upon her when she stopped.

"You needn't be; I shall stand close by, and your ma will be there."

After the handkerchief was tied about her eyes, Nurse led Effie up some steps, and placed her on a high platform, where something like leaves touched her head, and the soft snap of lamps seemed to fill the air.

Music began as soon as Nurse clapped her hands, the voices outside sounded nearer, and the tramp was evidently coming up the stairs.

"Now, my precious, look and see how you and your dear ma have made a merry Christmas for them that needed it!"

Off went the bandage; and for a minute Effie really did think she was asleep again, for she actually stood in "a grove of Christmas trees," all gay and shining as in her vision. Twelve on a side, in two rows down the room, stood the little pines, each on its low table; and behind Effie a taller one rose to the roof, hung with wreaths of popcorn, apples, oranges, horns of candy, and cakes of all sorts, from sugary hearts to gingerbread Jumbos. On the smaller trees she saw many of her own discarded toys and those Nursey bought, as well as heaps that seemed to have rained down straight from that delightful Christmas country where she felt as if she were again.

"How splendid! Who is it for? What is that noise? Where is mamma?" cried Effie, pale with pleasure and surprise, as she stood looking down the brilliant little street from her high place.

Before Nurse could answer, the doors at the lower end flew open, and in marched twenty-four little blue-gowned orphan girls, singing sweetly, until amazement changed the song to cries of joy and wonder as the shining spectacle appeared. While they stood staring with round eyes at the wilderness of pretty things about them, mamma stepped up beside Effie, and holding her hand fast to give her courage, told the story of the dream in a few simple words, ending in this way:—

"So my little girl wanted to be a Christmas spirit too, and make this a happy day for those who had not as many pleasures and comforts as she has. She likes surprises, and we planned this for you all. She shall play the good fairy, and give each of you something from this tree, after which every one will find her own name on a small tree, and can go to enjoy it in her own way. March by, my dears, and let us fill your hands."

Nobody told them to do it, but all the hands were clapped heartily before a single child stirred; then one by one they came to look up wonderingly at the pretty giver of the feast as she leaned down to offer them great yellow oranges, red apples, bunches of grapes, bonbons, and cakes, till all were gone, and a double row of smiling faces turned toward her as the children filed back to their places in the orderly way they had been taught.

Then each was led to her own tree by the good ladies who had helped mamma with all their hearts; and the happy hubbub that arose would have satisfied even Santa Claus himself,— shrieks of joy, dances of delight, laughter and tears (for some tender little things could not bear so much pleasure at once, and sobbed with mouths full of candy and hands full of toys). How they ran to show one another the new treasures! how they peeped and tasted, pulled and pinched, until the air was full of queer noises, the floor covered with papers, and the little trees left bare of all but candles!

"I don't think heaven can be any gooder than this," sighed one small girl, as she looked about her in a blissful maze, holding her full apron with one hand, while she luxuriously carried sugar-plums to her mouth with the other.

"Is that a truly angel up there?" asked another, fascinated by the little white figure with the wreath on its shining hair, who in some mysterious way had been the cause of all this merry-making.

"I wish I dared to go and kiss her for this splendid party," said a lame child, leaning on her crutch, as she stood near the steps, wondering how it seemed to sit in a mother's lap, as Effie was doing, while she watched the happy scene before her.

Effie heard her, and remembering Tiny Tim, ran down and put her arms about the pale child, kissing the wistful face, as she said sweetly "You may; but mamma deserves the thanks. She did it all; I only dreamed about it."

Lame Katy felt as if "a truly angel" was embracing her, and could only stammer out her thanks, while the other children ran to see the pretty spirit, and touch her soft dress, until she stood in a crowd of blue gowns laughing as they held up their gifts for her to see and admire.

Mamma leaned down and whispered one word to the older girls; and suddenly they all took hands to dance round Effie, singing as they skipped.

It was a pretty sight, and the ladies found it hard to break up the happy revel; but it was late for small people, and too much fun is a mistake. So the girls fell into line, and marched before Effie and mamma again, to say goodnight with such grateful little faces that the eyes of those who looked grew dim with tears. Mamma kissed every one; and many a hungry childish heart felt as if the touch of those tender lips was their best gift. Effie shook so many small hands that her own tingled; and when Katy came she pressed a small doll into Effie's hand, whispering, "You didn't have a single present, and we had lots. Do keep that; it's the prettiest thing I got."

"I will," answered Effie, and held it fast until the last smiling face was gone, the surprise all

over, and she safe in her own bed, too tired and happy for anything but sleep.

"Mamma, it *was* a beautiful surprise, and I thank you so much! I don't see how you did it; but I like it best of all the Christmases I ever had, and mean to make one every year. I had my splendid big present, and here is the dear little one to keep for love of poor Katy; so even that part of my wish came true."

And Effie fell asleep with a happy smile on her lips, her one humble gift still in her hand, and a new love for Christmas in her heart that never changed through a long life spent in doing good.

Down Pens

SAKI

"Have you written to thank the Froplinsons for what they sent us?" asked Egbert.

"No," said Janetta, with a note of tired defiance in her voice; "I've written eleven letters today expressing surprise and gratitude for sundry unmerited gifts, but I haven't written to the Froplinsons."

"Someone will have to write to them," said Egbert.

"I don't dispute the necessity, but I don't think the someone should be me," said Janetta. "I wouldn't mind writing a letter of angry recrimination or heartless satire to some suitable recipient; in fact, I should rather enjoy it, but I've come to the end of my capacity for expressing servile amiability. Eleven letters today and nine yesterday, all couched in the same strain of ecstatic thankfulness: really, you can't expect me to sit down to another. There is such a thing as writing oneself out."

"I've written nearly as many," said Egbert, "and I've had my usual business correspondence to get through too. Besides, I don't know what it was that the Froplinsons sent us."

"A William the Conqueror calendar," said Janetta, "with a quotation of one of his great thoughts for every day in the year."

"Impossible," said Egbert, "he didn't have three hundred and sixty-five thoughts in the whole of his life, or, if he did, he kept them to himself. He was a man of action, not of introspection."

"Well, it was William Wordsworth, then," said Janetta; "I know William came into it somewhere."

"That sounds more probable," said Egbert; "well, let's collaborate on this letter of thanks and get it done. I'll dictate, and you can scribble it down. 'Dear Mrs. Froplinson—thank you and your husband so much for the very pretty calendar you sent us. It was very good of you to think of us.' "

"You can't possibly say that," said Janetta, laying down her pen.

"It's what I always do say, and what everyone says to me," protested Egbert.

"We sent them something on the twenty-second," said Janetta, "so they simply had to think of us. There was no getting away from it."

"What did we send them?" asked Egbert gloomily.

"Bridge-markers," said Janetta, "in a cardboard case, with some inanity about 'digging for fortune with a royal spade' emblazoned on the cover. The moment I saw it in the shop I said to myself 'Froplinsons' and to the attendant 'How much?' When he said 'Ninepence!' I gave him their address, jabbed our card in, paid tenpence or elevenpence to cover the postage, and thanked heaven. With less sincerity and infinitely more trouble they eventually thanked me."

"The Froplinsons don't play bridge," said Egbert.

"One is not supposed to notice social deformities of that sort," said Janetta; "it wouldn't be polite. Besides, what trouble did they take to find out whether we read Wordsworth with gladness? For all they knew or cared we might be frantically embedded in the belief that all poetry begins and ends with John Masefield, and it might infuriate or depress us to have a daily sample of Wordsworthian products flung at us."

"Well, let's get on with the letter of thanks," said Egbert.

"Proceed," said Janetta.

" 'How clever of you to guess that Wordsworth is our favourite poet,' " dictated Egbert.

Again Janetta laid down her pen.

"Do you realize what that means?" she asked; "a Wordsworth booklet next Christmas, and another calendar the Christmas after, with the same problem of having to write suitable letters of thankfulness. No, the best thing to do is to drop all further allusion to the calendar and switch off on to some other topic."

"But what other topic?"

"Oh, something like this: 'What do you think of the New Year Honours List? A friend of ours made such a clever remark when he read it.' Then you can stick in any remark that comes into your head; it needn't be clever. The Froplinsons won't know whether it is or isn't."

"We don't even know on which side they are in politics," objected Egbert; "and anyhow you can't suddenly dismiss the subject of the calendar. Surely there must be some intelligent remark that can be made about it."

"Well, we can't think of one," said Janetta wearily; "the fact is, we've both written ourselves out. Heavens! I've just remembered Mrs. Stephen Ludberry. I haven't thanked her for what she sent."

"What did she send?"

"I forget; I think it was a calendar."

There was a long silence, the forlorn silence of those who are bereft of hope and have almost ceased to care.

Presently Egbert started from his seat with an air of resolution. The light of battle was in his eyes.

"Let me come to the writing table," he exclaimed.

"Gladly," said Janetta. "Are you going to write to Mrs. Ludberry or the Froplinsons?"

"To neither," said Egbert, drawing a stack of note-paper towards him; "I'm going to write to the editor of every enlightened and influential newspaper in the Kingdom. I'm going to suggest that there should be a sort of epistolary Truce of God during the festivities of Christmas and New Year. From the twenty-fourth of December to the third or fourth of January it shall be considered an offence against good sense and good feeling to write or expect any letter or communication that does not deal with the necessary events of the moment. Answers to invitations, arrangements about trains, renewal of club subscriptions, and, of course, all the ordinary everyday affairs of business, sickness, engaging new cooks, and so forth, these will be dealt with in the usual manner as something inevitable, a legitimate part of our daily life. But all the devastating accretions of correspondence, incident to the festive season, these should be swept away to give the season a chance of being really festive, a time of untroubled, unpunctuated peace and good will."

"But you would have to make some acknowledgment of presents received," objected Janetta; "otherwise people would never know whether they had arrived safely."

"Of course, I have thought of that," said Egbert; "every present that was sent off would be accompanied by a ticket bearing the date of dispatch and the signature of the sender, and some conventional hieroglyphic to show that it was intended to be a Christmas or New Year gift; there would be a counterfoil with space for the recipient's name and the date of arrival, and all you would have to do would be to sign and date the counterfoil, add a conventional hieroglyphic indicating heartfelt thanks and gratified surprise, put the thing into an envelope and post it."

"It sounds delightfully simple," said Janetta wistfully, "but people would consider it too cut-and-dried, too perfunctory."

"It is not a bit more perfunctory than the present system," said Egbert; "I have only the same conventional language of gratitude at my disposal with which to thank dear old Colonel Chuttle for his perfectly delicious Stilton, which we shall devour to the last morsel, and the Froplinsons know that we are bored with their calen-

dar, whatever we may say to the contrary, just as we know that they are bored with the bridge-markers in spite of their written assurance that they thanked us for our charming little gift. What is more, the Colonel knows that even if we had taken a sudden aversion to Stilton or been forbidden it by the doctor, we should still have written a letter of hearty thanks around it. So you see the present system of acknowledgment is just as perfunctory as the counterfoil business would be, only ten times more tiresome and brain-racking."

"Your plan would certainly bring the ideal of a Happy Christmas a step nearer realization," said Janetta.

"There are exceptions, of course," said Egbert, "people who really try to infuse a breath of reality into their letters of acknowledgment. Aunt Susan, for instance, who writes: 'Thank you very much for the ham; not such a good flavor as the one you sent last year, which itself was not a particularly good one. Hams are not what they used to be.' It would be a pity to be deprived of her Christmas comments, but that loss would be swallowed up in the general gain."

"Meanwhile," said Janetta, "what *am* I to say to the Froplinsons?"

The Worst Christmas Story

CHRISTOPHER MORLEY

We had been down to an East Side settlement house on Christmas afternoon. I had watched my friend Dove Dulcet, in moth-riddled scarlet and cotton wool trimmings, play Santa Claus for several hundred adoring urchins and their parents. He had done this for many years, but I had never before seen him insist on the amiable eccentricity of returning uptown still wearing the regalia of the genial saint. But Dove is always unusual, and I thought—as did the others who saw him, in the subway and elsewhere—it was a rather kindly and innocent concession to the hilarity of the day.

When we had got back to his snug apartment he beamed at me through his snowy fringes of false whisker, and began rummaging in the tall leather boots of his costume. From each one he drew a bottle of chianti.

"From a grateful parent on Mulberry Street," he said. "My favorite bootlegger lives down that way, and I've been playing Santa to his innumerable children for a number of years. The garb attributed—quite inaccurately, I expect—to Saint Nicholas of Bari, has its uses. Even the keenest revenue agent would hardly think of holding up poor old Santa."

He threw off his trappings, piled some logs on the fire, and we sat down for our annual celebration. Dove and I have got into the habit of spending Christmas together. We are both old bachelors, with no close family ties, and we greatly enjoy the occasion. It isn't wholly selfish, either, for we usually manage to spice our fun with a little unexpected charity in some of the less fortunate quarters of the town.

As my friend uncorked the wicker-bound bottles I noticed a great pile of Christmas mail on his table.

"Dove, you odd fish," I said. "Why don't you open your letters? I should have thought that part of the fun of Christmas is hurrying to look through the greetings from friends. Or do you leave them to the last, to give them greater savor?"

He glanced at the heap, with a curious expression on his face.

"The Christmas cards?" he said. "I postpone them as long as I possibly can. It's part of my penance."

"What on earth do you mean?"

He filled two glasses, passed one to me, and sat down beside the cheerful blaze.

"Here's luck, old man!" he said. "Merry Christmas."

I drank with him, but something evasive in his manner impelled me to repeat my question.

"What a ferret you are, Ben!" he said. "Yes, I put off looking at the Christmas cards as long as I dare. I suppose I'll have to tell you. It's one of the few skeletons in my anatomy of melancholy that you haven't exhumed. It's a queer kind of Christmas story."

He reached over to the table, took up a number of the envelopes, and studied their handwritings. He tore them open one after another, and read the enclosed cards.

"As I expected," he said. "Look here, it's no use your trying to make copy out of this yarn. No editor would look at it. It runs counter to all the good old Christmas tradition."

"My dear Dove," I said, "if you've got a Christmas story that's 'different,' you've got

something that editors will pay double for."

"Judge for yourself," he said. From the cards in his lap he chose four and gave them to me. "Begin by reading those."

Completely mystified, I did so.

The first showed a blue bird perched on a spray of holly. The verse read:

> Our greeting is "Merry Christmas!"
> None better could we find,
> And tho' you are now out of sight,
> You're ever in our mind.

The second card said, below a snow scene of mid-Victorian characters alighting from a stage coach at the hospitable door of a country mansion:

> Should you or your folk ever call at our door
> You'll be welcome, we promise you—nobody more;
> We wish you the best of the Joy and Cheer
> That can come with Christmas and last through the year!

The third, with a bright picture of three stout old gentlemen in scarlet waistcoats, tippling before an open fire:

> Jolly old Yule, Oh the jolly old Yule
> Blesses rich man and poor man and wise man and fool—
> Be merry, old friend, in this bright winter weather,
> And you'll Yule and I'll Yule, we'll all Yule together!

The fourth—an extremely ornate vellum leaflet, gilded with Oriental designs and magi on camels—ran thus:

> I pray the prayer the Easterners do;
> May the Peace of Allah abide with you—
> Through days of labor and nights of rest
> May the love of Allah make you blest.

"Well," I said, "of course I wouldn't call them great poetry, but the sentiments are generous enough. Surely it's the spirit in which they're sent that counts. It doesn't seem like you to make fun—"

Dulcet leaned forward. "Make fun?" he said. "Heavens, I'm not making fun of them. The ghastly thing is, I wrote those myself."

There was nothing to say, so I held my peace.

"You didn't know, I trust, that at one time I was regarded as the snappiest writer of greeting sentiments (so the trade calls them) in the business? That was long ago, but the sentiments themselves, and innumerable imitations of them, go merrily on. You see, out of the first ten cards that I picked up, four are my own composition. Can you imagine the horror of receiving, every Christmas, every New Year, every Easter, every birthday, every Halloween, every Thanksgiving, cards most of which were written by yourself? And when I think of the honest affection with which those cards were chosen for me by my unsuspecting friends, and contrast their loving simplicity with—"

He broke off, and refilled the glasses.

"I told you," he said, "that this was the worst Christmas story in the world! But I must try to tell it a little better, at any rate. Well, it has some of the traditional ingredients.

"You remember the winter of the Great Panic—1906, wasn't it? I had a job in an office downtown, and was laid off. I applied everywhere for work—nothing doing. I had been writing a little on the side, verses and skits for the newspapers, but I couldn't make enough that way to live on. I had an attic in an old lodging house on Gay Street. (The Village was still genuine then, no hokum about it.) I used to reflect on the irony of that name, Gay Street, when I was walking about trying not to see the restaurants, they made me feel so hungry. I still get a queer feeling in the pit of my stomach when I pass by Gonfarone's—there was a fine thick savor of spaghetti and lentil soup that used to float out from the basement as I went along Eighth Street.

"There was a girl in it too, of course. You'll smile when I tell you who she was. Peggy Cassell,

who does the magazine covers. Yes, she's prosperous enough now—so are we all. But those were the days!

"It's the old bachelors who are the real sentimentalists, hey? But by Jove, how I adored that girl! She was fresh from upstate somewhere, studying at the League, and doing small illustrating jobs to make ends approach. I was as green and tender as she. I was only twenty-five, you know. To go up to what Peggy called her studio—which was only a bleak bedroom she shared with another girl—and smoke cigarettes and see her wearing a smock and watch her daub away at a thing she intended to be a 'portrait' of me, was my idea of high tide on the seacoast of Bohemia. Peggy would brew cocoa in a chafing dish and then the other girl would tactfully think

of some errand, and we'd sit, timidly and uncomfortably, with our arms around each other, and talk about getting married some day, and prove by Cupid's grand old logarithms that two can live cheaper than one. I used to recite to her that ripping old song 'My Peggy is a young thing, And I'm not very auld,' and it would knock us both cold.

"The worst of it was, poor Peggy was almost as hard up as I was. In fact, we were both so hard up that I'm amazed we didn't get married, which is what people usually do when they have absolutely no prospects. But with all her sweet sentiment Peggy had a streak of sound caution. And as a matter of fact, I think she was better off than I was, because she did get a small allowance from home. Anyway, I was nearly desperate, tearing

my heart out over the thought of this brave little creature facing the world for the sake of her art, and so on. She complained of the cold, and I remember taking her my steamer rug off my own bed, telling her I was too warm. After that I used to shingle myself over with newspapers when I went to bed. It was bitter on Gay Street that winter.

"But I said this was a Christmas Story. So it is. It began like this. About Hallowe'en I had a little poem in *Life*—nothing of any account, but a great event to me, my first appearance in Big Time journalism. Well, one day I got a letter from a publisher in Chicago asking permission to reprint it on a card. He said also that my verses had just the right touch which was needed in such things, and that I could probably do some 'holiday greetings' for him. He would be glad to see some Christmas 'sentiments,' he said, and would pay one dollar each for any he could use.

"You can imagine that it didn't take me long to begin tearing off sentiments though I stipulated, as a last concession to my honor, that my name should not be used. There was no time to lose: it was now along in November, and these things—to be sold to the public for Christmas a year later—must be submitted as soon as possible so that they could be illustrated and ready for the salesmen to take on the road in January.

"Picture, then, the young author of genial greeting cards, sitting ironically in the chilliest attic on Gay Street—a dim and draughty little elbow of the city—and attempting to ignite his wits with praise of the glowing hearth and the brandied pudding. The room was heated only by a small gas stove, one burner of which had been scientifically sealed by the landlady; an apparatus, moreover, in which asphyxia was the partner of warmth. When that sickly sweetish gust became too overpotent, see the author throw up the window and retire to bed, meditating under a mountain of news-print further applause of wintry joy and fellowship. I remember one sentiment—very likely it is among the pile on the table here: it is a great favorite—which went:

May blazing log and steaming bowl
And wreaths of mistletoe and holly
Remind you of a kindred soul
Whose love for you is warm and jolly!

My, how cold it was the night I wrote that."

Dove paused, prodded the logs to a brighter flame, and leaned closer to the chimney as though feeling a reminiscent chill.

"Well, as Christmas itself drew nearer, I became more and more agitated. I had sent in dozens of these compositions; each batch was duly acknowledged, and highly praised. The publisher was pleased to say that I had a remarkable aptitude for 'greetings'; my Christmas line, particularly, he applauded as being full of the robust and hearty spirit of the old-fashioned Yule. My Easter touch, he felt, was a little thin and tepid by comparison. So I redoubled my metrical cheer. I piled the logs higher and higher upon my imaginary hearth; I bore in cups of steaming wassail; blizzards drummed at my baronial window panes; stage coaches were halted by drifts axle-deep; but within the circle of my mid-Victorian halloo, all was mirth: beauty crowded beneath the pale mistletoe; candles threw a tawny shine; the goose was carved and the port wine sparkled. And all the while, if you please, it was December of the panic winter; no check had yet arrived from the delighted publisher; I had laid aside other projects to pursue this golden phantom; I ate once a day, and sometimes kept warm by writing my mellow outbursts of gladness in the steam-heated lobbies of hotels.

"I had said nothing to Peggy about this professional assumption of Christmas heartiness. For one thing, I had talked to her so much, and with such youthful ardor, of my literary ambitions and ideals, that I feared her ridicule; for another, my most eager hope was to surprise her with an opulent Christmas present. She, poor dear, was growing a trifle threadbare too; she had spoken, now and then, of some sort of fur neckpiece she had seen in shop windows; this, no less, was my secret ambition. And so, as the streets grew

brighter with the approach of the day, and still the publisher delayed his remittance, I wrote him a masterly letter. It was couched in the form of a Christmas greeting from me to him; it acknowledged the validity of his contention that he had postponed a settlement because I was still submitting more and more masterpieces and he planned to settle en bloc; but it pointed out the supreme and tragic irony of my having to pass a Christmas in starvation and misery because I had spent so

much time dispersing altruistic and factitious good will.

"As I waited anxiously for a reply, I was further disquieted by distressing behavior on Peggy's part. She had been rather strange with me for some time, which I attributed partly to my own shabby appearance and wretched preoccupation with my gruesome task. She had rallied me— some time before—on my mysterious mien, and I may have been clumsy in my retorts. Who can

always know just the right accent with which to chaff a woman? At any rate, she had—with some suddenly assumed excuse of propriety—forbidden me the hospitality of her bedroom studio; even my portrait (which we had so blithely imagined as a national triumph in future years when we both stood at the crest of our arts) had been discontinued. We wandered the streets together, quarrelsome and unhappy; we could agree about nothing. In spite of this, I nourished my hopeful secret, still believing that when my check came, and enabled me to mark the Day of Days with the coveted fur, all would be happier than ever.

"It was two days before Christmas, and you may elaborate the picture with all the traditional tints of Dickens pathos. It was cold and snowy and I was hungry, worried, and forlorn. I was walking along Eighth Street wondering whether I could borrow enough money to telegraph to Chicago. Just by the Brevoort I met Peggy, and to my chagrin and despair she was wearing a beautiful new fur neckpiece—a tippet, I think they used to call them in those days. She looked a different girl: her face was pink, her small chin nestled adorably into the fur collar, her eyes were bright and merry. Well, I was only human, and I guess I must have shown my wretched disappointment. Of course she hadn't known that I hoped to surprise her in just that way, and when I blurted out something to that effect, she spoke tartly.

" 'You!' she cried. 'How could you buy me anything like that? I suppose you'd like me to tramp around in the snow all winter and catch my death of cold!'

"In spite of all the Christmas homilies I had written about good will and charity and what not, I lost my temper.

" 'Ah,' I said bitterly, 'I see it all now! I wasn't prosperous enough, so you've found someone else who can afford to buy furs for you. That's why you've kept me away from the studio, eh? You've got some other chap on the string.'

"I can still see her little flushed face, rosy with wind and snow, looking ridiculously stricken as she stood on that wintry corner. She began to say

something, but I was hot with the absurd rage of youth. All my weeks of degradation on Gay Street suddenly boiled up in my mind. I was grotesquely melodramatic and absurd.

" 'A rich lover!' I sneered. 'Go ahead and take him! I'll stick to poverty and my ideals. You can have the furs and fleshpots!'

"Well, you never know how a woman will take things. To my utter amazement, instead of flaming up with anger, she burst into tears. But I was too proud and troubled to comfort her.

" 'Yes, you're right,' she sobbed. 'I had such fine dreams, but I couldn't stick it out. I'm not worthy of your ideals. I guess I've sold myself.' She turned and ran away down the slippery street, leaving me flabbergasted.

"I walked around and around Washington Square, not knowing what to do. She had as good as admitted that she had thrown me over for some richer man. And yet I didn't feel like giving her up without a struggle. Perhaps it all sounds silly now, but it was terribly real then.

"At last I went back to Gay Street. On the hall table was a letter from the publisher, with a check for fifty dollars. He had accepted fifty of the hundred or so pieces I had sent, and said if I would consider going to Chicago he would give me a position on his staff as Assistant Greeting Editor. 'Get into a good sound business,' he wrote. 'There will never be a panic in the Greeting line.'

"When I read that letter I was too elated to worry about anything. I would be able to fix things with Peggy somehow. I would say to her, in a melting voice, 'My Peggy is a young thing,' and she would tumble. She must love me still, or she wouldn't have cried. I rushed round to her lodging house, and went right upstairs without giving her a chance to deny me. I knocked, and when she came to the door she looked frightened and ill. She tried to stop me, but I burst in and waved the letter in front of her.

" 'Look at this, Peggy darling!' I shouted. 'We're going to be rich and infamous. I didn't tell you what I was doing, because I was afraid you'd be ashamed of me, after all my talk about high

ideals. But anything is better than starving and freezing on Gay Street, or doing without the furs that pretty girls need.'

"She read the letter, and looked up at me with the queerest face.

" 'Now no more nonsense about the other man,' I said. 'I'll buy you a fur for Christmas that'll put his among camphor balls. Who is he, anyway?'

"She surprised me again, for this time she began to laugh.

" 'It's the same one,' she said. 'I mean, the same publisher—your friend in Chicago. Oh Dove, I've been doing drawings for Christmas cards, and I think they must be yours.'

"It was true. Her poor little cold studio was littered with sketches for Christmas drawings— blazing fires and ruddy Georgian squires with tankards of hissing ale and girls in sprigged muslin being coy under the mistletoe. And when she showed me the typewritten verses the publisher had sent her to illustrate, they were mine, sure enough. She had had her check a day sooner than I, and had rushed off to buy herself the fur her heart yearned for.

" 'I was so ashamed of doing the work,' she said—with her head on my waistcoat—'that I didn't dare tell you.' "

Dove sighed, and leaned back in his chair. A drizzle of rain and sleet tinkled on the window pane, but the fire was a core of rosy light.

"Not much of a Christmas story, eh?" he said. "Do you wonder, now, that I hesitate to look back at the cards I wrote and Peggy illustrated?"

"But what happened?" I asked. "It seems a nice enough story as far as you've gone."

"Peggy was a naughty little hypocrite," he said. "I found out that she wasn't really ashamed of illustrating my Greetings at all. She thought they were lovely. She honestly did. And presently she told me she simply couldn't marry a man who would capitalize Christmas. She said it was too sacred."

O Little Town of Bethlehem

Phillips Brooks (1835–1893)

Lewis H. Redner (1831–1908)

R.F.

1. O lit - tle town of Beth - le - hem, How still we _ see thee lie! A -
2. For Christ is born of Ma - ry, And gath - ered _ all a - bove, While

bove thy deep and dream - less sleep The si - lent _ stars go by; Yet
mor - tals sleep, the an - gels keep Their watch of _ won - d'ring love. O

in thy dark streets shin - eth The ev - er - last - ing Light; The
morn - ing stars, to - geth - er Pro - claim the ho - ly birth, And

hopes and fears of all the years Are met in thee to - night.
prais - es sing to God the King, And peace to men on earth!

3. How silently, how silently,
   The wondrous gift is giv'n!
   So God imparts to human hearts
   The blessings of His heav'n.
   No ear may hear His coming,
   But in this world of sin,
   Where meek souls will receive Him still,
   The Dear Christ enters in.

4. O holy Child of Bethlehem,
   Descend to us, we pray;
   Cast out our sin and enter in;
   Be born in us today!
   We hear the Christmas angels
   The great glad tidings tell;
   O come to us, abide with us
   Our Lord Emmanuel!

We Three Kings of Orient Are

John Henry Hopkins, Jr. (1820–1891)
Simply and without dragging

John Henry Hopkins, Jr.

1. We three kings of O - ri - ent are, Bear - ing
5. Glo - rious now be - hold Him a - rise, King, and

gifts we tra - verse a - far, Field and foun - tain,
God, and sac - ri - fice; Heaven sings al - le -

moor and moun - tain, Fol - low - ing yon - der star.
lu - ia: Al - le - lu - ia the earth re - plies. O —

REFRAIN AFTER EACH VERSE:

Star of won - der, star of night, Star with

roy - al beau - ty bright, West - ward lead - ing,

still pro - ceed - ing, Guide us to thy per - fect light.

GASPAR. 2. Born a King on Beth-le-hem's plain, Gold I bring to
MELCHIOR. 3. Frank-in-cense to of-fer have I, In-cense owns a
BALTHASAR. 4. Myrrh is mine; its bit-ter per-fume Breathes a life of

crown Him a-gain, King for-ev-er, ceas-ing
De-i-ty nigh: Prayer and prais-ing all men
gath-er-ing gloom; Sor-rowing, sigh-ing, bleed-ing,

to Refrain

nev-er O-ver us all to reign. O ____
rais-ing, Wor-ship Him, God on high. O ____
dy-ing, Sealed in the stone-cold tomb. O ____

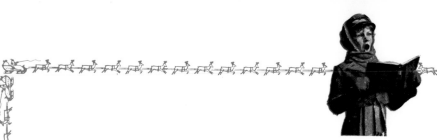

What Child Is This?

William Chatterton Dix (1837-1898)
With Motion

16th-century English
R.F.

1. What Child is this, _ Who, laid to rest, _ On Ma-ry's lap _ is sleep - ing?Whom
2. Why lies He in _ such mean es - tate_Where ox and ass _ are feed - ing? Good
3. So bring Him in - cense, gold, and myrrh, Come,peas-ant,king _ to own Him; The

an - gels greet_ with an - thems sweet, _ While shep - herds watch _ are keep - ing?
Chris - tian,fear: _ for sin - ners here _ The si - lent Word _ is plead - ing.
King of kings_ sal - va - tion brings, _ Let lov - ing hearts _ en - throne him.

REFRAIN:

This, this _ is Christ the King, _Whom shep-herds guard_ and an - gels sing:

This, this _ is Christ the King, _ The Babe, _ the Son _ of Ma - ry.

It Came upon a Midnight Clear

Edmund H. Sears (1810–1876)
Flowing but not too fast

Richard S. Willis (1819–1900)
R.F.

1. It came up-on a mid-night clear, That glo-rious song of old, _____ From an-gels bend-ing near the earth To touch their harps of gold; _____ "Peace on the earth, good will to men, From heav'n's all-gra-cious King." _____ The

2. Still through the clo-ven skies they come, With peace-ful wings un-furled, _____ And still their heav'n-ly mu-sic floats O'er all the wea-ry world; _____ A-bove its sad and low-ly plains They bend on hov-'ring wing, _____ And

world in sol - emn still - ness lay To hear the an - gels sing. __
ev - er o'er__ its Ba - bel sounds The bless - ed an - gels sing. __

3. O ye, beneath life's crushing load,
   Whose forms are bending low,
   Who toil along the climbing way,
   With painful steps and slow,
   Look now, for glad and golden hours
   Come swiftly on the wing:
   O rest beside the weary road,
   And hear the angels sing!

4. For lo! the days are hast'ning on,
   By prophets seen of old,
   When with the ever circling years,
   Shall come the time foretold,
   When the new heav'n and earth shall own
   The Prince of Peace their King,
   And the whole world send back the song
   Which now the angels sing.

Silent Night

Joseph Mohr (1792–1848)

Franz Xavier Gruber (1787–1863)

H.W.S.

Serenely

1. Si - lent night, ho - ly night! All is calm, all is bright Round yon Vir - gin Moth - er and Child. Ho - ly In - fant so ten - der and mild,

1. Stil - le Nacht, hei - li - ge Nacht! Al - les schläft, ein - sam wacht Nur das trau - te hoch - hei - li - ge Paar, Hol - der Kna - be mit lok - ki - gem Haar.

Sleep in heav-en-ly peace, ____ Sleep in heav-en-ly peace.

Schlaf in himm-li-scher Ruh, ____ Schlaf in himm-li-scher Ruh!

omit for last stanza

Hark! the Herald Angels Sing

Charles Wesley (1707–1788)

Felix Mendelssohn-Bartholdy (1809–1847)

R.F.

With festal pomp

1. Hark! the her - ald an - gels sing, __ "Glo - ry to the new - born King;
2. Christ, by high - est heaven a - dored; __ Christ, the ev - er - last - ing Lord;

Peace on earth, and mer - cy mild, __ God and sin - ners rec - on - ciled!"
Come, De - sire of Na - tions, come, __ Fix in us thy hum - ble home.

Joy - ful, all ye na - tions, rise, __ Join the tri - umph of the skies; __
Veiled in flesh the God - head see; __ Hail th'In - car - nate De - i - ty, __

With th'an - gel - ic hosts pro - claim, "Christ is ___ born in Beth - le - hem!"
Pleased as man with man to dwell; Je - sus, ___ our Em - man - u - el.

REFRAIN:

Hark! the her - ald an - gels sing, "Glo - ry ___ to the new-born King."

3. Hail, the heav'n-born Prince of Peace!
   Hail, the Sun of Righteousness!
   Light and life to all He brings,
   Ris'n with healing in His wings;
   Mild He lays His glory by,
   Born that man no more may die,
   Born to raise the sons of earth,
   Born to give them second birth;
                              Refrain:

Angels We Have Heard on High

Les Anges dans nos campagnes

Traditional French

Swiftly, joyously

Traditional French

H.W.S.

An - gels we have heard on high,_ Sweet - ly sing - ing o'er the plains,
Les an - ges dans nos cam-pa-gnes Ont en - ton - né l'hymne des cieux;

And the _ moun-tains _ in re - ply. Ech - o - ing their _ joy - ous strains.
Et l'é - cho de nos mon-ta-gnes Re - dit _ ce chant _ mé - lo-dieux:

Glo - - - - - - - - - - - - - - - ri - a

2. Shepherds, why this jubilee?
   Why your joyous strains prolong?
   What the gladsome tidings be
   Which inspire your heav'nly song?
   Gloria in excelsis Deo,
   Gloria in excelsis Deo.

3. Come to Bethlehem and see
   Him whose birth the angels sing;
   Come, adore on bended knee,
   Christ the Lord, the newborn King.
   Gloria in excelsis Deo,
   Gloria in excelsis Deo.

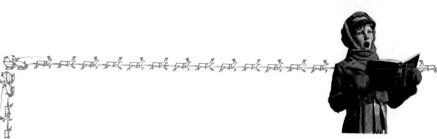

The First Nowell

Traditional

Traditional
H.W.S.

1. The first Now - ell, the an - gel did say, Was to
2. They look - ed up and saw a star Shin - ing

cer - tain poor shep - herds in fields as they lay; In fields where
in the east, be - yond them far, And to the

they lay keep - ing their sheep, On a cold win - ter's night that
earth it gave great light, And so it con - tin - ued both

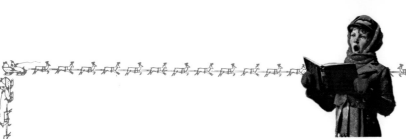

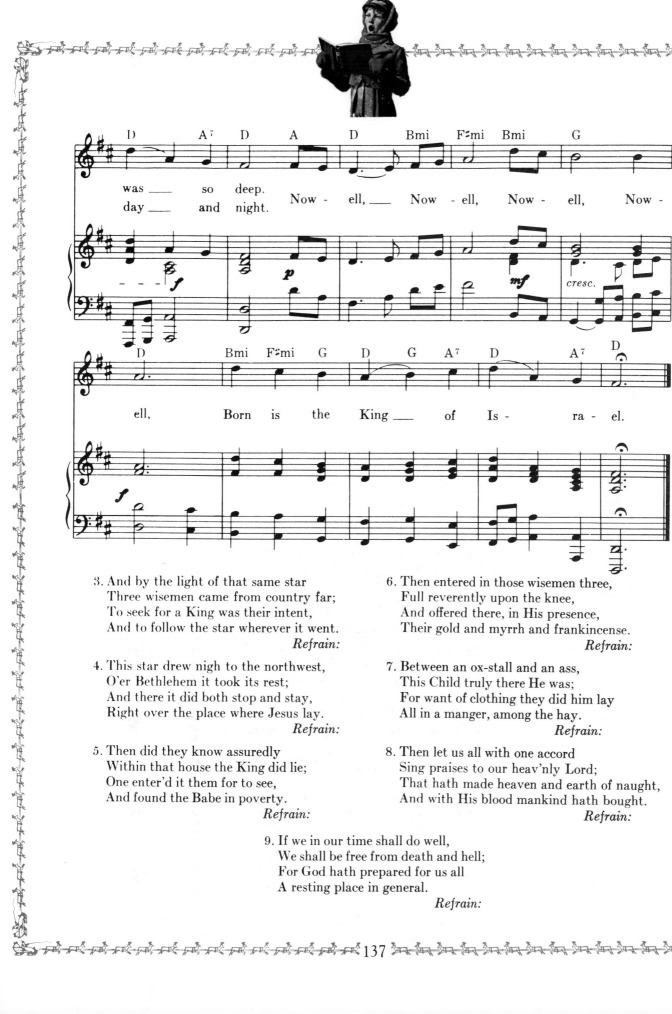

was ___ so deep.
day ___ and night. Now - ell, ___ Now - ell, Now - ell, Now -

ell, Born is the King ___ of Is - ra - el.

3. And by the light of that same star
   Three wisemen came from country far;
   To seek for a King was their intent,
   And to follow the star wherever it went.
   Refrain:

4. This star drew nigh to the northwest,
   O'er Bethlehem it took its rest;
   And there it did both stop and stay,
   Right over the place where Jesus lay.
   Refrain:

5. Then did they know assuredly
   Within that house the King did lie;
   One enter'd it them for to see,
   And found the Babe in poverty.
   Refrain:

6. Then entered in those wisemen three,
   Full reverently upon the knee,
   And offered there, in His presence,
   Their gold and myrrh and frankincense.
   Refrain:

7. Between an ox-stall and an ass,
   This Child truly there He was;
   For want of clothing they did him lay
   All in a manger, among the hay.
   Refrain:

8. Then let us all with one accord
   Sing praises to our heav'nly Lord;
   That hath made heaven and earth of naught,
   And with His blood mankind hath bought.
   Refrain:

9. If we in our time shall do well,
   We shall be free from death and hell;
   For God hath prepared for us all
   A resting place in general.
   Refrain:

Joy to the World!

Isaac Watts (1674–1748)

Unknown
R.F.

Vigorously

1. Joy to the world! the Lord is come; Let earth re-ceive her King; Let
2. Joy to the world! the Sav-iour reigns; Let men their songs em-ploy; While
3. He rules the world with truth and grace, And makes the na-tions prove The

ev-'ry heart pre-pare Him room, And heav'n and na-ture sing, And
fields and floods, rocks, hills and plains Re-peat the sound-ing joy, Re-
glo-ries of His right-eous-ness, And won-ders of His love, And

heav'n and na-ture sing, And heav'n, and heav'n and na-ture sing.
peat the sound-ing joy, Re-peat, re-peat the sound-ing joy.
won-ders of His love, And won-ders, and won-ders of His love.

The Twelve Days of Christmas

Traditional English

Traditional English
R.F.

1. On the first day of Christ - mas my true love sent to me A

par - tridge in a pear tree.

2. On the se - cond
3. On the third day of Christ - mas my true love sent to me
4. On the fourth

F   C⁷   F   B♭   F   C⁷   F   *D.S.* 𝄋

Two   tur-tle   doves   and   a   par-tridge __ in   a   pear   tree.
Three   French hens, (two *etc.*)
Four   call-ing birds, (three *etc.*)

repeat as necessary

D.S. 𝄋

F   C⁷   F

5. On   the   fifth   day   of   Christ-mas my   true love sent   to   me

F   Bdim   C⁷

Five   gold _____ rings!

⊕ F   Gmi⁷

5-12. Four __ call-ing birds, three   French   hens,

two — tur-tle doves, And a par-tridge — in a pear tree.

6. On the sixth
7. On the sev-enth
8. On the eighth
9. On the ninth day of Christ-mas my true love sent to me
10. On the tenth
11. On the elev-enth
12. On the twelfth

(Last time)

Six geese a-lay-ing, Five gold _____ rings!
Sev-en swans a-swim-ming (six *etc.*)
Eight maids a-milk-ing (seven *etc.*)
Nine la-dies danc-ing (eight *etc.*)
Ten lords a-leap-ing (nine *etc.*)
Elev-en pi-pers pi-ping (ten *etc.*)
Twelve drum-mers drum-ming (eleven *etc.*)

repeat as necessary

O Come, All Ye Faithful

(?) John Francis Wade (1712–1786)

(?) John Reading (d. 1692)

R.F.

O come, all ye faith-ful, joy-ful and tri-um-phant, O
Ad - es - te, fi - de - les, lae - ti, tri - um - phan - tes, Ve -

come ye, O come _ ye to Beth - le - hem;
ni - te, ve - ni - te in Beth - le - hem:

Come and be-hold Him, born the King of an - gels; O
Na - tum vi - de - te Re - gem an - ge - lo - rum: Ve -

come, let us a- dore Him, O come, let us a- dore Him, O
ni- te a- do- re- mus, ve- ni- te a- do- re- mus, Ve-

come, let us a- dore Him,___ Christ,___ the Lord!
ni- te a- do- re- mus ___ Do- mi- num.

2. Sing, choirs of angels, sing in exultation,
   O sing, all ye citizens of heaven above!
   Glory to God, all glory in the highest;
   O come, let us adore Him,
   O come, let us adore Him,
   O come, let us adore Him, Christ, the Lord!

3. Yea, Lord, we greet Thee, born this happy morning,
   Jesus, to Thee be all glory giv'n;
   Word of the Father, now in flesh appearing;
   O come, let us adore Him,
   O come, let us adore Him,
   O come, let us adore Him, Christ, the Lord!

2. *Cantet nunc Io chorus angelorum,*
   Cantet nunc aula caelestium:
   Gloria, gloria in excelsis Deo:
   Venite adoremus, venite adoremus,
   Venite adoremus Dominum.

3. *Ergo qui natus die hodierna,*
   Iesu, tibi sit gloria:
   Patris aeterni verbum caro factum:
   Venite adoremus, venite adoremus,
   Venite adoremus Dominum.

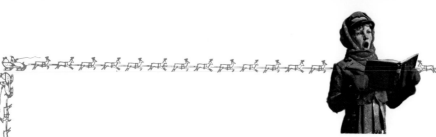

God Rest You Merry, Gentlemen

ti - dings of com - fort and joy, com - fort and joy; O ___

ti - dings of com - fort and joy.

3. From God our heav'nly Father
   A blessed angel came;
   And unto certain shepherds
   Brought tidings of the same;
   How that in Bethlehem was born
   The son of God by name.
   Refrain:

4. "Fear not, then," said the angel,
   "Let nothing you affright,
   This day is born a Saviour
   Of a pure Virgin bright,
   To free all those who trust in Him
   From Satan's power and might."
   Refrain:

5. The shepherds at those tidings
   Rejoicéd much in mind,
   And left their flocks a-feeding,
   In tempest, storm, and wind,
   And went to Bethl'em straightway
   This blessed Babe to find.
   Refrain:

6. But when to Bethlehem they came.
   Whereat this Infant lay,
   They found Him in a manger,
   Where oxen feed on hay;
   His mother Mary kneeling,
   Unto the Lord did pray.
   Refrain:

7. Now to the Lord sing praises,
   All you within this place,
   And with true love and brotherhood
   Each other now embrace;
   This holy tide of Christmas
   All others doth deface.
   Refrain:

8. God bless the ruler of this house,
   And send him long to reign,
   And many a merry Christmas
   May live to see again;
   Among your friends and kindred
   That live both far and near—
   And God send you a happy new year, happy new year,
   And God send you a happy new year.

Deck the Halls with Boughs of Holly

Traditional Welsh

Traditional Welsh
H.W.S.

1. Deck the halls with boughs of hol - ly,
2. See the blaz - ing yule be - fore us, Fa - la - la - la - la, la - la - la - la;
3. Fast a - way the old year pass - es.

'Tis the sea - son to be jol - ly,
Strike the harp and join the cho - rus, Fa - la - la - la - la, la - la - la - la.
Hail the new, ye lads and lass - es,

Don we now our gay ap - par - el,
Fol - low me in mer - ry mea - sure, Fa - la - la, fa - la - la, la - la - la.
Sing we joy - ous songs to - geth - er,

Troll the an-cient Christ-mas car - ol,
While I tell of Christ-mas trea - sure, Fa-la-la-la-la, la-la-la-la!
Heed - less of the wind and weath-er,

with octaves ad lib. _ _ _ _ _ _ _ _ _ _ _

Go Tell It on the Mountain

Negro Spiritual
Lively

Negro Spiritual
R.F.

1. When I was a seek-er, I sought both night and day, I
2. He made me a watch-man up-on the cit-y wall, And

sought the Lord to help me, and He showed me the way,
if I am a Chris-tian, I am the least of all. Oh!

March time (a little slower)

Go tell it on the moun-tain, o-ver the hills and

Jingle Bells

John Pierpont (1785–1866)

John Pierpont
R.F.

Dash - ing through the snow, In a one - horse o - pen sleigh,

O'er the fields we go, Laugh - ing all the way;

Bells on bob - tail ring, Mak - ing spir - its bright, What

fun   it   is   to   ride   and   sing   A   sleigh - ing   song   to - night!

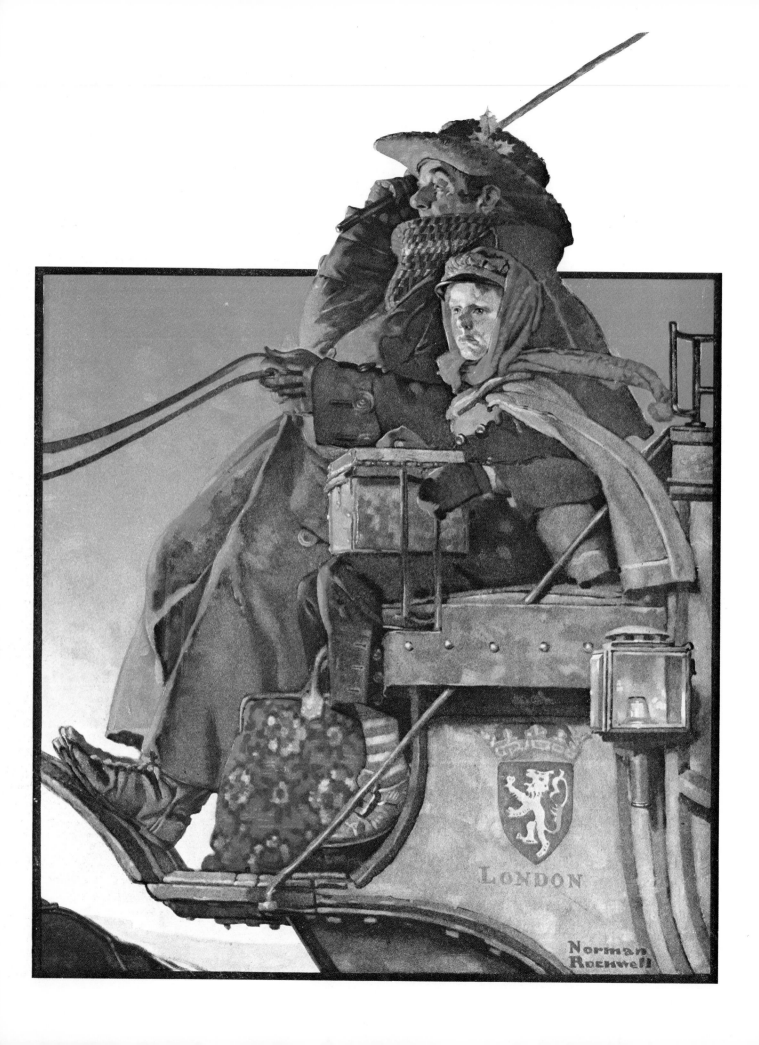

Christmas Trees

A CHRISTMAS CIRCULAR LETTER

ROBERT FROST

The city had withdrawn into itself
And left at last the country to the country;
When between whirls of snow not come to lie
And whirls of foliage not yet laid, there drove
A stranger to our yard, who looked the city,
Yet did in country fashion in that there
He sat and waited till he drew us out,
A-buttoning coats, to ask him who he was.
He proved to be the city come again
To look for something it had left behind
And could not do without and keep its Christmas.
He asked if I would sell my Christmas trees;
My woods—the young fir balsams like a place
Where houses all are churches and have spires.
I hadn't thought of them as Christmas trees.
I doubt if I was tempted for a moment
To sell them off their feet to go in cars
And leave the slope behind the house all bare,
Where the sun shines now no warmer than the moon.
I'd hate to have them know it if I was.
Yet more I'd hate to hold my trees, except
As others hold theirs or refuse for them,
Beyond the time of profitable growth—
The trial by market everything must come to.
I dallied so much with the thought of selling.
Then whether from mistaken courtesy
And fear of seeming short of speech, or whether
From hope of hearing good of what was mine,
I said, "There aren't enough to be worth while."

POEMS

"I could soon tell how many they would cut,
You let me look them over."

                    "You could look.
But don't expect I'm going to let you have them."
Pasture they spring in, some in clumps too close
That lop each other of boughs, but not a few
Quite solitary and having equal boughs
All round and round. The latter he nodded "Yes" to,
Or paused to say beneath some lovelier one,
With a buyer's moderation, "That would do."
I thought so too, but wasn't there to say so.
We climbed the pasture on the south, crossed over,
And came down on the north.

                    He said, "A thousand."

"A thousand Christmas trees!—at what apiece?"

He felt some need of softening that to me:
"A thousand trees would come to thirty dollars."

Then I was certain I had never meant
To let him have them. Never show surprise!
But thirty dollars seemed so small beside
The extent of pasture I should strip, three cents
(For that was all they figured out apiece)—
Three cents so small beside the dollar friends
I should be writing to within the hour
Would pay in cities for good trees like those,
Regular vestry-trees whole Sunday Schools
Could hang enough on to pick off enough.

A thousand Christmas trees I didn't know I had!
Worth three cents more to give away than sell
As may be shown by a simple calculation.
Too bad I couldn't lay one in a letter.
I can't help wishing I could send you one,
In wishing you herewith a Merry Christmas.

Christmas in a Village

JOHN CLARE

Each house is swept the day before,
And windows stuck with evergreens;
The snow is besomed from the door,
And comfort crowns the cottage scenes.
Gilt holly with its thorny pricks
And yew and box with berries small,
These deck the unused candlesticks,
And pictures hanging by the wall.

Neighbours resume their annual cheer,
Wishing with smiles and spirits high
Glad Christmas and a happy year
To every morning passer-by.
Milkmaids their Christmas journeys go
Accompanied with favoured swain,
And children pace the crumping snow
To taste their granny's cake again.

Hung with the ivy's veining bough,
The ash trees round the cottage farm
Are often stripped of branches now
The cottar's Christmas hearth to warm.
He swings and twists his hazel band,
And lops them off with sharpened hook,
And oft brings ivy in his hand
To decorate the chimney nook...

The shepherd now no more afraid
Since custom doth the chance bestow
Starts up to kiss the giggling maid
Beneath the branch of mistletoe
That 'neath each cottage beam is seen
With pearl-like berries shining gay,
The shadow still of what hath been
Which fashion yearly fades away.

And singers too, a merry throng,
At early morn with simple skill
Yet imitate the angel's song
And chant their Christmas ditty still;
And 'mid the storm that dies and swells
By fits—in hummings softly steals
The music of the village bells
Ringing round their merry peals.

And when it's past, a merry crew
Bedecked in masks and ribbons gay,
The morris dance their sports renew
And act their winter evening play.
The clown turned king for penny praise
Storms with the actor's strut and swell,
And harlequin a laugh to raise
Wears his hunchback and tinkling bell.

And oft for pence and spicy ale
With winter nosegays pinned before,
The wassail singer tells her tale
And drawls her Christmas carols o'er,
While prentice boy with ruddy face
And rime-bepowdered dancing locks
From door to door with happy pace
Runs round to claim his Christmas box.

Christmas Eve in Our Village

PHYLLIS McGINLEY

Main Street is gay. Each lamppost glimmers,
  Crowned with a blue, electric star.
The gift tree by our fountain shimmers,
  Superbly tall, if angular
  (Donated by the Men's Bazaar).

With garlands proper to the times
  Our doors are wreathed, our lintels strewn.
From our two steeples sound the chimes,
  Incessant, through the afternoon,
  Only a little out of tune.

Breathless, with boxes hard to handle,
  The grocery drivers come and go.
Madam the Chairman lights a candle
  To introduce our club's tableau.
  The hopeful children pray for snow.

They cluster, mittened, in the park
  To talk of morning, half affrighted,
And early comes the winter dark
  And early are our windows lighted
  To beckon homeward the benighted.

The eggnog's lifted for libation,
  Silent at last the postman's ring,
But on the plaza near the station
  The carolers are caroling.
  "O Little Town!" the carolers sing.

Christmas Eve at Sea

JOHN MASEFIELD

A wind is rustling "south and soft,"
    Cooing a quiet country tune,
The calm sea sighs, and far aloft
    The sails are ghostly in the moon.

Unquiet ripples lisp and purr,
    A block there pipes and chirps i' the sheave,
The wheel-ropes jar, the reef-points stir
    Faintly—and it is Christmas Eve.

The hushed sea seems to hold her breath,
    And o'er the giddy, swaying spars,
Silent and excellent as Death,
    The dim blue skies are bright with stars.

Dear God—they shone in Palestine
    Like this, and yon pale moon serene
Looked down among the lowing kine
    On Mary and the Nazarene.

The angels called from deep to deep,
    The burning heavens felt the thrill,
Startling the flocks of silly sheep
    And lonely shepherds on the hill.

To-night beneath the dripping bows,
    Where flashing bubbles burst and throng,
The bow-wash murmurs and sighs and soughs
    A message from the angels' song.

The moon goes nodding down the west,
    The drowsy helmsman strikes the bell;
Rex Judaeorum natus est,
    I charge you, brothers, sing *Nowell,*
Nowell,
Rex Judaeorum natus est.

A Visit from St. Nicholas

CLEMENT CLARKE MOORE

'Twas the night before Christmas, when all through the house
Not a creature was stirring, not even a mouse.
The stockings were hung by the chimney with care,
In hopes that St. Nicholas soon would be there.
The children were nestled all snug in their beds,
While visions of sugar-plums danced in their heads;
And mamma in her kerchief, and I in my cap,
Had just settled our brains for a long winter's nap—
When out on the lawn there arose such a clatter
I sprang from my bed to see what was the matter.
Away to the window I flew like a flash,
Tore open the shutter, and threw up the sash.
The moon on the breast of the new-fallen snow
Gave a lustre of midday to objects below;
When what to my wondering eye should appear
But a miniature sleigh and eight tiny reindeer,
With a little old driver, so lively and quick,
I knew in a moment it must be St. Nick!
More rapid than eagles his coursers they came,
And he whistled and shouted and called them by name.
"Now, Dasher! now, Dancer! now, Prancer and Vixen!
On, Comet! on, Cupid! on, Donder and Blitzen!—
To the top of the porch, to the top of the wall,
Now, dash away, dash away, dash away all!"
As dry leaves that before the wild hurricane fly,
When they meet with an obstacle mount to the sky,
So, up to the housetop the coursers they flew,
With a sleigh full of toys—and St. Nicholas, too.
And then, in a twinkling, I heard on the roof
The prancing and pawing of each little hoof.
As I drew in my head and was turning around,
Down the chimney St. Nicholas came with a bound:
He was dressed all in fur from his head to his foot,
And his clothes were all tarnished with ashes and soot:
A bundle of toys he had flung on his back,
And he looked like a peddler just opening his pack.

His eyes, how they twinkled! his dimples, how merry!
His cheeks were like roses, his nose like a cherry;
His droll little mouth was drawn up like a bow,
And the beard on his chin was as white as the snow.
The stump of a pipe he held tight in his teeth,
And the smoke, it encircled his head like a wreath.
He had a broad face and a little round belly
That shook, when he laughed, like a bowl full of jelly.
He was chubby and plump—a right jolly old elf:
And I laughed when I saw him, in spite of myself;
A wink of his eye, and a twist of his head,
Soon gave me to know I had nothing to dread.
He spoke not a word, but went straight to his work,
And filled all the stockings: then turned with a jerk,
And laying his finger aside of his nose,
And giving a nod, up the chimney he rose.
He sprang to his sleigh, to his team gave a whistle,
And away they all flew like the down of a thistle.
But I heard him exclaim, ere they drove out of sight,
"Happy Christmas to all, and to all a good-night!"

Christmas Greeting from a Fairy to a Child

LEWIS CARROLL

Lady, dear, if Fairies may
　　For a moment lay aside
Cunning tricks and elfish play,
　　'Tis at happy Christmas-tide.

We have heard the children say—
　　Gentle children, whom we love—
Long ago on Christmas Day,
　　Came a message from above.

Still, as Christmas-tide comes round,
　　They remember it again—
Echo still the joyful sound,
　　"Peace on earth, good-will to men!"

Yet the hearts must childlike be
　　Where such heavenly guests abide;
Unto children, in their glee,
　　All the year is Christmas-tide!

Thus, forgetting tricks and play
　　For a moment, Lady dear,
We would wish you, if we may,
　　Merry Christmas, glad New Year!

Ceremonies for Christmas

ROBERT HERRICK

Come, bring with a noise,
My merry, merry boys,
The Christmas log to the firing;
While my good dame, she
Bids ye all be free;
And drink to your heart's desiring.

With the last year's brand
Light the new block, and
For good success in his spending,
On your psalteries play,
That sweet luck may
Come while the log is a-tending.

Drink now the strong beer,
Cut the white loaf here,
The while the meat is shredding;
For the rare mince-pie
And the plums stand by
To fill the paste that's a-kneading.

The Mahogany Tree

WILLIAM MAKEPEACE THACKERAY

Christmas is here:
Winds whistle shrill,
Icy and chill,
Little care we:
Little we fear
Weather without,
Sheltered about
The Mahogany Tree.

Once on the boughs
Birds of rare plume
Sang, in its bloom;
Night-birds are we:
Here we carouse,
Singing like them,
Perched round the stem
Of the jolly old tree.

Here let us sport,
Boys, as we sit;
Laughter and wit
Flashing so free.
Life is but short—
When we are gone,
Let them sing on,
Round the old tree.

Evenings we knew,
Happy as this;
Faces we miss,
Pleasant to see.
Kind hearts and true,
Gentle and just,
Peace to your dust!
We sing round the tree.

Care, like a dun,
Lurks at the gate:
Let the dog wait;
Happy we'll be!
Drink, every one;
Pile up the coals,
Fill the red bowls,
Round the old tree!

Drain we the cup.—
Friend, art afraid?
Spirits are laid
In the Red Sea.
Mantle it up;
Empty it yet;
Let us forget,
Round the old tree.

Sorrows, begone!
Life and its ills,
Duns and their bills,
Bid we to flee.
Come with the dawn,
Blue-devil sprite,
Leave us to-night,
Round the old tree.

The Boy Who Laughed at Santa Claus

OGDEN NASH

In Baltimore there lived a boy.
He wasn't anybody's joy.
Although his name was Jabez Dawes,
His character was full of flaws.
In school he never led the classes,
He hid old ladies' reading glasses,
His mouth was open while he chewed,
And elbows to the table glued.
He stole the milk of hungry kittens,
And walked through doors marked No Admittance.

He said he acted thus because
There wasn't any Santa Claus.
Another trick that tickled Jabez
Was crying "Boo!" at little babies.
He brushed his teeth, they said in town,
Sideways instead of up and down.
Yet people pardoned every sin
And viewed his antics with a grin
Till they were told by Jabez Dawes,
"There isn't any Santa Claus!"
Deploring how he did behave,
His parents quickly sought their grave.
They hurried through the portals pearly,
And Jabez left the funeral early.
Like whooping cough, from child to child,
He sped to spread the rumor wild:
"Sure as my name is Jabez Dawes
There isn't any Santa Claus!"
Slunk like a weasel or a marten
Through nursery and kindergarten,
Whispering low to every tot,
"There isn't any, no, there's not!
No beard, no pipe, no scarlet clothes,
No twinkling eyes, no cherry nose,
No sleigh, and furthermore, by Jiminy,
Nobody coming down the chimney!"
The children wept all Christmas Eve
And Jabez chortled up his sleeve.
No infant dared to hang up his stocking
For fear of Jabez' ribald mocking.
He sprawled on his untidy bed,
Fresh malice dancing in his head,
When presently with scalp a-tingling,
Jabez heard a distant jingling;
He heard the crunch of sleigh and hoof
Crisply alighting on the roof.
What good to rise and bar the door?
A shower of soot was on the floor.
Jabez beheld, oh, awe of awes,
The fireplace full of Santa Claus!

Then Jabez fell upon his knees
With cries of "Don't," and "Pretty please."
He howled, "I don't know where you read it.
I swear some other fellow said it!"
"Jabez," replied the angry saint,
"It isn't I, it's you that ain't.
Although there *is* a Santa Claus,
There isn't any Jabez Dawes!"
Said Jabez then with impudent vim,
"Oh, yes there is; and I am him!
Your language don't scare me, it doesn't—"
And suddenly he found he wasn't!
From grinning feet to unkempt locks
Jabez became a jack-in-the-box,
An ugly toy in Santa's sack,
Mounting the flue on Santa's back.
The neighbors heard his mournful squeal;
They searched for him, but not with zeal.
No trace was found of Jabez Dawes,
Which led to thunderous applause,
And people drank a loving cup
And went and hung their stockings up.
All you who sneer at Santa Claus,
Beware the fate of Jabez Dawes,
The saucy boy who told the saint off;
The child who got him, licked his paint off.

Mistletoe

WALTER DE LA MARE

Sitting under the mistletoe
(Pale-green, fairy mistletoe),
One last candle burning low,
All the sleepy dancers gone,
Just one candle burning on,
Shadows lurking everywhere:
Some one came, and kissed me there.

Tired I was; my head would go
Nodding under the mistletoe
(Pale-green, fairy mistletoe),
No footsteps came, no voice, but only,
Just as I sat there, sleepy, lonely,
Stooped in the still and shadowy air
Lips unseen—and kissed me there.

Well, so that is that

W.H. AUDEN

Well, so that is that. Now we must dismantle the tree,
Putting the decorations back into their cardboard boxes—
Some have got broken—and carrying them up to the attic.
The holly and mistletoe must be taken down and burnt,
And the children got ready for school. There are enough
Left-overs to do, warmed up, for the rest of the week—
Not that we have much appetite, having drunk such a lot,
Stayed up so late, attempted—quite unsuccessfully—
To love all our relatives, and in general
Grossly overestimated our powers. Once again
As in previous years we have seen the actual Vision and
    failed
To do more than entertain it as an agreeable
Possibility, once again we have sent Him away
Begging though to remain His disobedient servant,
The promising child who cannot keep His word for long.

Yule's Come, and Yule's Gane

ANONYMOUS

Yule's come, and Yule's gane,
And we hae feasted weel,
Sae Jock maun to his flail again,
And Jenny to her wheel.

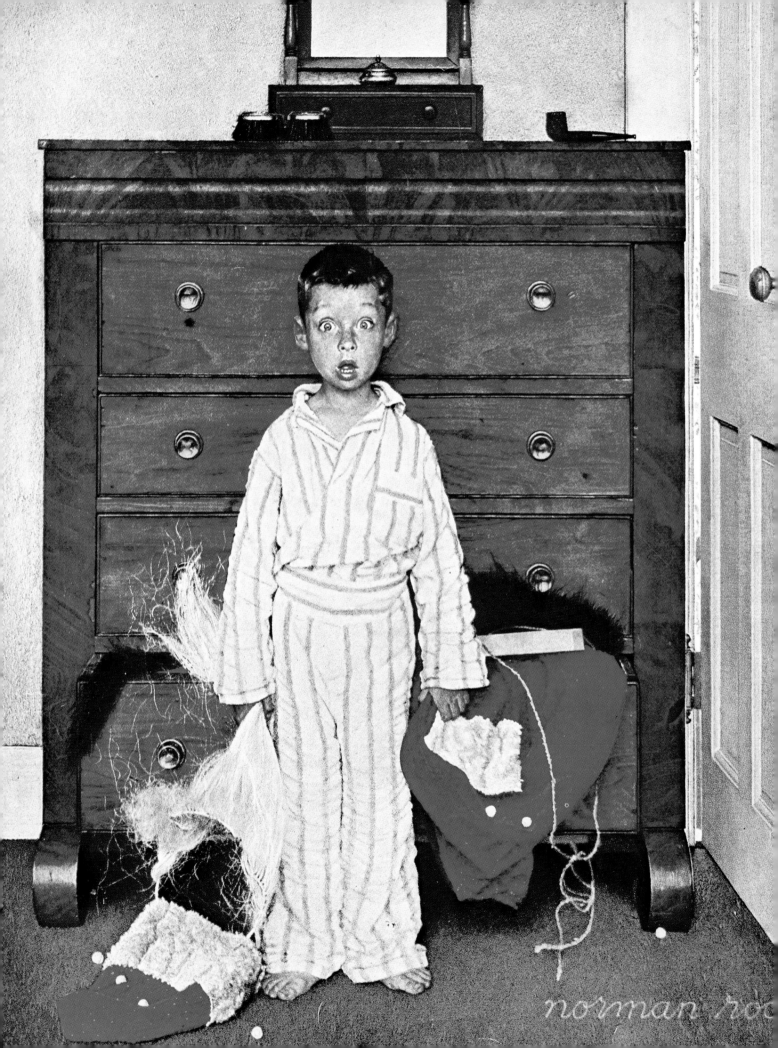

norman roc

Yes, Virginia,
There Is a Santa Claus

FRANCIS P. CHURCH

Dear Editor: I am 8 years old.
    Some of my little friends say there is no Santa
Claus.
    Papa says "If you see it in *The Sun* it's so."
    Please tell me the truth; is there a Santa Claus?
Virginia O'Hanlon

Virginia, your little friends are wrong. They have been affected by the skepticism of a skeptical age. They do not believe except they see. They think that nothing can be which is not comprehensible by their little minds. All minds, Virginia, whether they be men's or children's, are little. In this great universe of ours man is a mere insect, an ant, in his intellect, as compared with the boundless world about him, as measured by the intelligence capable of grasping the whole of truth and knowledge.

Yes, Virginia, there is a Santa Claus. He exists as certainly as love and generosity and devotion exist, and you know that they abound and give to your life its highest beauty and joy. Alas! how dreary would be the world if there were no Santa Claus! It would be as dreary as if there were no Virginias. There would be no childlike faith then, no poetry, no romance to make tolerable this existence. We should have no enjoyment, except in sense and sight. The eternal light with which childhood fills the world would be extinguished.

Not believe in Santa Claus! You might as well not believe in fairies! You might get your papa to hire men to watch in all the chimneys on Christmas Eve to catch Santa Claus, but even if they did not see Santa Claus coming down, what would that prove? Nobody sees Santa Claus, but that is no sign that there is no Santa Claus. The most real things in the world are those that neither children nor men can see.

No Santa Claus! Thank God, he lives, and he lives forever. A thousand years from now, Virginia, nay, ten times ten thousand years from now, he will continue to make glad the heart of childhood.

—*The New York Sun*, September 21, 1897

189

Once on Christmas

DOROTHY THOMPSON

It is Christmas Eve—the festival that belongs to mothers and fathers and children, all over the so-called Western world. It's not a time to talk about situations, or conditions, or reactions, or people who emerge briefly into the news. My seven-year-old son asked me this evening to tell him what Christmas was like when I was a little girl, before people came home for Christmas in airplanes, thirty odd years ago. And so I told him this:

A long, long time ago, when your mother was your age, and not nearly as tall as you, she lived with her mother, and father, and younger brother, and little sister, in a Methodist parsonage, in Hamburg, New York. It was a tall wooden house, with a narrow verandah on the side, edged with curley-cues of woodwork at the top, and it looked across a lawn at the church where father preached every Sunday morning and evening. In the backyard there were old Baldwin and Greening apple trees, and a wonderful, wonderful barn. But that is another story. The village now has turned into a suburb of the neighboring city of Buffalo, and fathers who work there go in and out every day on the trains and buses, but then it was just a little country town, supported by the surrounding farms.

Father preached in his main church there on Sunday mornings but in the afternoons he had to drive out to the neighboring village of Armor where there was just a little box of a church in the middle of the farming country. For serving both parishes, he received his house and one thousand dollars a year. But he didn't always get the thousand dollars. Sometimes the crops were bad, and the farmers had no money, and when the farmers had no money the village people didn't have any either. Then the farmers would come to us with quarters of beef, or halves of pigs, or baskets of potatoes, and make what they called a donation. My mother hated the word, and sometimes would protest, but my father would laugh, and say, "Let them pay in what they can! We are all in the same boat together."

For weeks before Christmas we were very, very busy. Mother was busy in the kitchen, cutting up citron and sorting out raisins and clarifying suet for the Christmas pudding—and shooing all of us out of the room, when we crept in to snatch a raisin, or a bit of kernel from the butter-nuts that my little brother was set to cracking on the woodshed floor, with an old-fashioned flat-iron.

I would lock myself into my little bed-room, to bend over a handkerchief that I was hemstitching for my mother. It is very hard to hemstitch when you are seven years old, and the thread would knot, and break, and then one would have to begin again, with a little rough place, where one had started over. I'm afraid the border of that handkerchief was just one succession of knots and starts.

The home-made presents were only a tiny part of the work! There was the Christmas tree! Mr. Heist, from my father's Armor parish, had brought it from his farm, a magnificent hemlock, that touched the ceiling. We were transported with admiration, but what a tree to trim! For there was no money to buy miles of tinsel and boxes of colored glass balls.

But in the pantry was a huge stone jar of popcorn. When school was over, in the afternoons,

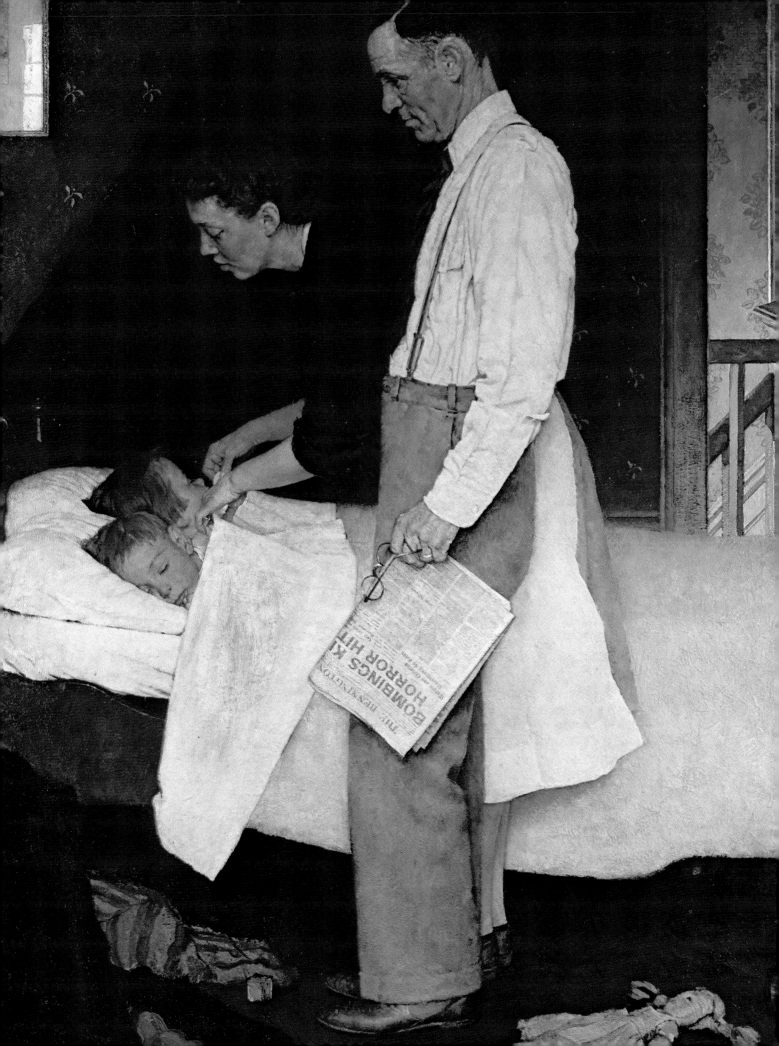

we all gathered in the back parlor, which was the family sitting room. The front parlor was a cold place, where portraits of John Wesley and Frances Willard hung on the walls, and their eyes, I remember, would follow a naughty child accusingly around the room. The sofas in that room were of walnut, with roses and grapes carved on their backs, just where they'd stick into your back, if you fidgeted in them, and were covered with horse-hair which was slippery when it was new, and tickly when it was old. But that room was given over to visits from the local tycoons who sometimes contributed to the church funds, and couples who came to be married.

The back parlor was quite, quite different. It had an ingrain carpet on the floor, with patterns of maple leaves, and white muslin curtains at the windows, and an assortment of chairs contributed by the Parsonage Committee. A Morris chair, I remember, and some rockers, and a fascinating cabinet which was a desk and a bookcase, and a chest of drawers, and a mirror, all in one.

In this room there was a round iron stove, a very jolly stove, a cozy stove that winked at you with its red isin-glass eyes. On top of this stove was a round iron plate, it was flat, and a wonderful place to pop corn. There was a great copper kettle, used for making maple syrup, and we shook the popper on the top of the stove—first I shook until my arm was tired, and then Willard shook, until he was tired, and even the baby shook. The corn popped, and we poured it into the kettle and emptied the kettle, and poured it full again, until there was a whole barrel-full of popcorn, as white and fluffy as the snow that carpeted the lawn between the parsonage and the church.

Then we each got a darning needle, a big one, and a ball of string. We strung the popcorn into long, long ropes, to hang upon the tree. But that was only half of it! There were stars to be cut out of kindergarten paper, red and green, and silver, and gold, and walnuts to be wrapped in gold paper, or painted with gold paint out of the paint-box that I had been given for my birthday. One got the paint into one's finger-nails, and it smelled like bananas. And red apples to be polished, because a shiny apple makes a brave show on a tree. And when it was all finished, it was Christmas Eve.

For Christmas Eve we all wore our best clothes. Baby in a little challis dress as blue as her eyes, and I had a new pinafore of Swiss lawn that my Aunt Margaret had sent me from England. We waited, breathless, in the front parlor while the candles were lit.

Then my mother sat at the upright piano in a rose-red cashmere dress and played, and my father sang, in his lovely, pure, gay, tenor voice:

"It came upon the midnight clear
That glorious song of old,
From angels bending near the earth
To touch their harps of gold."

And then we all marched in. It is true that we had decorated the tree ourselves, and knew intimately everything on it, but it shone in the dark room like an angel, and I could see the angels bending down, and it was so beautiful that one could hardly bear it. We all cried, "Merry Christmas!" and kissed each other.

There were bundles under the tree, most alluring bundles! But they didn't belong to Christmas Eve. They were for the morning. Before the morning came three little children would sit sleepily in the pews of their father's church and hear words drowsily, and shift impatiently, and want to go to sleep in order to wake up very, very early!

And wake up early we did! The windows were still gray, and, oh, how cold the room was! The church janitor had come over at dawn to stoke the hot air furnace in the parsonage, but at its best it only heated the rooms directly above it, and the upstairs depended on grates in the floor, and the theory that heat rises. We shuddered out of our beds, trembling with cold and excitement, and into our clothes, which, when I was a little girl, were very complicated affairs indeed. First, a long fleece-lined union suit, and then a ferris waist dripping with buttons, then the cambric drawers edged with embroidery, and a flannel petticoat handsome with scallops, and another petticoat of cambric and embroidery, just for show, and over that a gay plaid dress, and a dainty pinafore. What polishing of cheeks, and what brushing of hair and then a grand tumble down the stairs into the warm, cozy back parlor.

Presents! There was my beloved Miss Jam-up with a brand new head! Miss Jam-up was once a sweet little doll, dears, who had become badly battered about the face in the course of too affectionate ministrations, and here she was again, with a new head altogether and new clothes, and eyes that open and shut. Scarfs and mittens from my mother's lively fingers. A doll house made from a wooden cracker box and odds and ends of wall paper, with furniture cut from stiff cardboard—and that was mother's work, too. And a new woolen dress, and new pinafores!

Under the tree was a book: *The Water Babies,* by Charles Kingsley. *To my beloved daughter Dorothy.*

Books meant sheer magic. There were no automobiles—none for Methodist ministers, in those days. No moving pictures. No radio. But inside the covers of books was everything, everything, that exists outside in the world today. Lovely, lovely words of poetry, that slipped like colored beads along a string; tales of rose-red cities, half as old as time. All that men can imagine, and construct, and make others imagine.

One couldn't read the book now. But there it lay, the promise of a perfect afternoon. Before one could get at it, one would go into the dining room. And what a dinner! This Christmas there was Turkey—with best wishes from one of my father's parishioners. And the pudding, steaming, and with two kinds of sauce. And no one to say, "No, dear, I think one helping is enough."

We glutted ourselves, we distended ourselves, we ate ourselves into a coma, so that we all had to lie down and have a nap.

Then, lying before the stove, propped on my elbows, I opened the covers of my Christmas book.

"Once upon a time there was a little chimney sweep, and his name was Tom. He lived in a great town of the North Country . . . in England."

How well I knew that North Country, with its rows on rows of dark stone houses, its mine pits, its poor workmen. From such a town my father had come, across the ocean, to this village in upstate New York. I forgot Christmas, forgot everything, except the fate of little Tom. What a book! It wasn't just a story. There was poetry in it. The words of the poems sang in my head, so that after all these years I can remember them:

> *When all the world is young, lad,*
> *And all the trees are green;*
> *And every goose, a swan, lad,*
> *And every lass a Queen;*
> *Then hey for boot and spur, lad,*
> *And round the world away;*
> *Young blood must have its course, lad,*
> *And every dog his day.*

The little girl lay and dreamed that all the world was wide and beautiful, filled only with hearts as warm and hands as tender, and spirits as generous as the only ones she had ever known . . . when she was seven years old.

I WISH YOU ALL A MERRY CHRISTMAS!
I WISH US ALL A WORLD AS KIND AS A
CHILD CAN IMAGINE IT!

Christmas on a Farm in New York

THEODORE LEDYARD CUYLER

As the visits of Santa Claus in the night could only be through the chimney, we hung our stockings where they would be in full sight. Three score and ten years ago such modern contrivances as steam pipes, and those unpoetical holes in the floor called 'hot-air registers', were as entirely unknown in our rural regions as gas-burners or telephones. We had a genuine fire-place in our kitchen, big enough to contain an enormous back-log, and broad enough for eight or ten people to form 'a circle wide' before it and enjoy the genial warmth.

The last process before going to bed was to suspend our stockings in the chimney jambs; and then we dreamed of Santa Claus, or if we awoke in the night, we listened for the jingling of his sleigh-bells. At the peep of day we were aroused by the voice of my good grandfather, who planted himself in the stairway and shouted in a stentorian tone, 'I wish you all a Merry Christmas!' The contest was as to who should give the salutation first, and the old gentleman determined to get the start on us by sounding his greeting to the family before we were out of our rooms. Then came a race for the chimney corner; all the stockings came down quicker than they had gone up. What could not be contained in them was disposed upon the mantelpiece, or elsewhere. I remember that I once received an autograph letter from Santa Claus, full of good counsels; and our coloured cook told me that she awoke in the night and, peeping into the kitchen, actually saw the veritable old visitor light a candle and sit down at the table and write it! I believed it all as implicitly as I believed the Ten Commandments, or the story of David and Goliath. . . .

Christmas in Maine

ROBERT P. TRISTRAM COFFIN

If you want to have a Christmas like the one we had on Paradise Farm when I was a boy, you will have to hunt up a saltwater farm on the Maine coast, with bays on both sides of it, and a road that goes around all sorts of bays, up over Misery Hill and down, and through the fir trees so close together that they brush you and your horse on both cheeks. That is the only kind of place a Christmas like that grows. You must have a clear December night, with blue Maine stars snapping like sapphires with the cold, and the big moon flooding full over Misery, and lighting up the snowy spruce boughs like crushed diamonds. You ought to be wrapped in a buffalo robe to your nose, and be sitting in a family pung, and have your breath trailing along with you as you slide over the dry, whistling snow. You will have to sing the songs we sang, "God Rest You Merry, Gentlemen" and "Joy to the World," and you will be able to see your songs around you in the air like blue smoke. That's the only way to come to a Paradise Christmas.

And you really should cross over at least one broad bay on the ice, and feel the tide rifts bounce you as the runners slide over them. And if the whole bay booms out, every now and then, and the sound echoes around the wooded islands for miles, you will be having the sort of ride we loved to take from town, the night before Christmas.

I won't insist on your having a father like ours to drive you home to your Christmas. One with a wide moustache full of icicles, and eyes like the stars of the morning. That would be impossible, anyway, for there has been only one of him in the world. But it is too bad, just the same. For you won't have the stories we had by the fireplace.

You won't hear about Kitty Wells who died beautifully in song just as the sun came over the tops of the eastern mountains and just after her lover had named the wedding day, and you will not hear how Kitty's departure put an end to his mastering the banjo:

> *"But death came in my cabin door*
> *And took from me my joy, my pride,*
> *And when they said she was no more,*
> *I laid my banjo down and cried."*

But you will be able to have the rooms of the farmhouse banked with emerald jewels clustered on bayberry boughs, clumps of everlasting roses with gold spots in the middle of them, tree evergreens, and the evergreen that runs all over the Maine woods and every so often puts up a bunch of palm leaves. And there will be rose-hips stuck in pine boughs. And caraway seeds in every crust and cookie in the place.

An aunt should be on hand, an aunt who believes in yarrow tea and the Bible as the two things needed to keep children well. She will read the Nativity story aloud to the family, hurrying over the really exciting parts that happened at the stable, and bearing down hard on what the angels had to say and the more edifying points that might be supposed to improve small boys who like to lie too long abed in the mornings. She will put a moral even into Christmas greens, and she will serve well as a counterirritant to the over-eating of mince pies. She will insist on all boys washing behind their ears, and that will keep her days full to the brim.

The Christmas tree will be there, and it will have a top so high that it will have to be bent over

and run along the ceiling of the sitting room. It will be the best fir tree of the Paradise forests, picked from ten thousand almost perfect ones, and every bough on it will be like old-fashioned fans wide open. You will have brought it home that very morning, on the sled, from Dragonfly Spring.

Dragonfly Spring was frozen solid to the bottom, and you could look down into it and see the rainbows where you dented it with your copper-toed boots, see whole ferns caught motionless in the crystal deeps, and a frog, too, down there, with hands just like a baby's on him. Your small sister—the one with hair like new honey laid open—in the middle of a honeycomb—had cried out, "Let's dig him up and take him home and warm his feet!" (She is the same sister who ate up all your more vivid pastel crayons when you were away at school, and then ate up all the things you had been pretty sure were toadstools in Bluejay Woods, when you were supposed to be keeping an eye on her, but were buried so deep in "Mosses from an Old Manse" that you couldn't have been dug up with horses and oxen.)

Your dog, Snoozer, who is a curious and intricate combination of many merry pugs and many mournful hound-dogs, was snuffling all the time, hot on the feather-stitching the mice had made from bush to bush while you were felling the Christmas tree. A red squirrel was taking a white-pine cone apart on a hemlock bough, and telling Snoozer what he thought of him and all other dogs, the hour or so you were there.

There will be a lot of aunts in the house besides the Biblical one. Aunts of every complexion and cut. Christmas is the one time that even the most dubious of aunts take on value. One of them can make up wreaths, another can make rock candy that puts a tremble on the heart, and still another can steer your twelve-seater bobsled—and turn it over, bottom up, with you all in just the right place for a fine spill.

There will be uncles, too, to hold one end of the molasses taffy you will pull sooner or later, yanking it out till it flashes and turns into cornsilk that almost floats in the air, tossing your end of it back and probably lassoing your uncle around his neck as you do it, and pulling out a new rope of solid honey.

The uncles will smoke, too, and that will be a help to all the younger brothers who have been smoking their acorn-pipes out in the wood-shed, and who don't want their breaths to give them away. The uncles will make themselves useful in other ways. They will rig up schooners no bigger than your thumb, with shrouds like cobwebs; they will mend the bob-sled, tie up cut fingers, and sew on buttons after you shin up to the cupola in the barn; and—if you get on the good side of them—they will saw you up so much birch wood that you won't have to lay hand to a bucksaw till after New Year's.

There will be cousins by the cart load. He-ones and she-ones. The size you can sit on, and the size that can sit on you. Enough for two armies, on Little Round Top and on Big, up in the haymow. You will play Gettysburg there till your heads are full of hay chaff that will keep six aunts busy cleaning it out. And then you will come in to the house and down a whole crock of molasses cookies—the kind that go up in peaks in the middle—which somebody was foolish enough to leave the cover off.

Every holiday that came along, in my father's house, was the gathering of an Anglo-Saxon clan. My father was built for lots of people 'round him. But Christmas was a whole assembly of the West Saxons! My father wanted people in squads. There were men with wide moustaches and men with smooth places on top of their heads, women wide and narrow. Cousins of the second and third water, even, were there. Hired men, too. They were special guests and had to be handled with kid gloves, as New England hired men must. They had to have the best of everything, and you could not find fault with them, as you could with uncles, if they smacked you for upsetting their coffee into their laps. Babies were underfoot in full cry. The older children hunted in packs. The table had to be pieced out with flour barrels and bread boards and ironing boards. It was a house's length from the head of the table, where your father sat and manufactured the roast up into slivers, to your mother dishing out the pork gravy. Whole geese disappeared on the way down. The Christmas cake, which had been left sweetly to itself for a month to age into a miracle, was a narrow isthmus when it got to Mother. But Mother always said that Christmas, to her, was watching other people eat. She was the kind of mother who claimed that the neck and the back of the chicken were the tastiest parts.

The prize goose, whom you had brought up by hand and called Oliver Cromwell, Old Ironsides, or some such distinguished title, was duly carved. And Father found his wishbone snow-white and you all applauded, for that meant lots of snow and two more months of coasting on your sleds. There were mince pies by the legion. And if Uncle Tom were there, a whole raccoon baked just for him and girt around with browned sweet potatoes. Mother's wild strawberry jam was there on deck, winking at you like rubies from the holes in tarts that melted away like bubbles in the mouth. That dinner was three hours in Beulah Land!

Of course, there will be an apple pudding at such a season. Steamed in a lard bucket, and cut open with a string. A sauce of oranges and lemons to make an ocean around each steaming volcano of suet and russet apples as it falls crumbling from the loop of twine. It will have to be steamed in the boiler, if your Christmas is to be the size of ours, and cooked in a ten-pound lard pail. Better use a cod line instead of the twine of other holidays, to parcel it out to the members of the clan.

The whole nation of you in the house will go from one thing to another. The secret of the best Christmases is everybody doing the same things all at the same time. You will all fall to and string cranberries and popcorn for the tree, and the bright lines each of you has a hold on will radiate from the tree like ribbons on a maypole. Every-

body will have needles and thread in the mouth, you will all get in each other's way, but that is the art of doing Christmas right. You will all bundle up together for a ride in the afternoon. You had better take the horse-sled, as the pung will not begin to hold you. And even then a dozen or so of assorted uncles and aunts and cousins will have to come trooping after through the deep snow, and wait for their turn on the straw in the sled. Smaller cousins will fall off over the sides in great knots and never be missed, and the hullabaloo will roar on and send the rabbits flying away through the woods, showing their bobbing scuts.

Everybody will hang presents on the tree at once, when the sun has dipped down into the spruces in the west and you are back home in the sitting-room. There will be no nonsense of tip-toeing up and edging a package on when nobody is looking. Everybody knows who is giving him what. There is no mystery about it. Aunt Ella has made rag dinahs for all hands and the cook—for all under fourteen years of age—and she does not care who knows it. The dinahs are all alike, except that those for the children whose lower garments are forked have forked red-flannel pants instead of red-flannel petticoats. They all have pearl button eyes and stocking toes for faces. There will be so many hands at work on the tree at once that the whole thing will probably go over two or three times, and it will be well to make it fast with a hawser or so.

And then you will turn right around and take the presents off again, the minute you have got them all on and have lighted the candles up. There will be no waiting, with small children sitting around with aching hearts. The real candles will be a problem, in all that mass of spills. Boughs will take fire here and there. But there will be plenty of uncles around to crush out the small bonfires in their big brown hands. All the same, it would be well to have an Uncle Thomas who can take up a live coal in his thumb and finger, and light his pipe from it, cool as a cucumber. Better turn the extinguishing of the tree over to him.

There will be boughten presents, to be sure—a turtle of cardboard in a glassed, dainty box, hung on springs and swimming for dear life with all four feet, and popguns with their barrels ringed and streaked with red and yellow lines. Why popguns should be painted like broomsticks is one of the mysteries, along with the blue paint you always find on Maine cartwheels. Somebody will probably get one of those Swiss music-boxes that will eke out a ghostly "Last Rose of Summer," if tenderly cranked. There should be those little bottles of transparent candies, with real syrup in them, which I used to live for through the years. And there must be a German doll for every last girl, with mountains of yellow hair and cheeks looking as if life were a continuous blowing of bubbles. Boughten things are all right.

But if it is going to be our kind of Christmas, most of the presents will be home-made. Socks knit by the aunt who swears only by useful gifts. You have seen those socks growing up from their white toes for the last two weeks. Wristers, always red. A box of Aunt Louise's candied orange peel that she will never let on to anybody how she makes. Your father will have made a sled for every mother's son and daughter of you, with a bluebird, or robin redbreast, more real than life, painted on each one and your name underneath. You will never have another present to match that, though you grow up and become Midases. Popcorn balls, big as muskmelons, will be common ware. They will be dripping with molasses, and will stick your wristers and socks and other treasures together.

But the pith of the party is not reached until the whole nation of you sits down in rocking chairs, or lies down on their bellies in front of the six-foot gulf of the fireplace. The presents are all stowed, heaped and tucked away, stuck fast with cornballs. The last lamps are out. The firelight dances on the ceiling. It lights up the steel engraving of Major McCullock leaping from Kentucky to Ohio, with ten thousand mounted redskins yelling and reining in their steeds behind him. It lights up Daniel Boone's daughters as they

lean away towards their boat's end and scream their silent screams and drop their water lilies, while Indian head after Indian head grins up at them from the river of the Dark and Bloody Ground.

All the babies will be hushed and put away. All the younger fry will be more than half asleep. The toasted cheese and red herring will go 'round. The herring, by the way—if you are worthy to wear my shoes after me—which you yourself have smoked with green oak, and have gotten your own two eyes so that they looked like two burnt holes in a blanket while doing it, and have hugely enjoyed every hour of it all.

Then you had best find a fair substitute for my father. Give him the best chair in the house— and the way to find *that* is to push the cat out of it—and let him tear! He will begin by telling you about such people as the brilliant young ladies of Philadelphia who had a piano too big to fit their house, so they put it on the porch and played on it through the open window. Then he will sit back

and work his way to the Caliph of Bagdad, who had a daughter so homely that she had to wear a sack on her head when her suitors came awooing, and how she fell down a well and made herself a great fortune, and won the handsomest husband that ever wore a turban. That story, by the way, you will not find in the "Arabian Nights" even though you look for it, as I have done, till you have gray hairs in your head.

The firelight will get into your father's eyes and on his hair. He will move on from Bagdad to Big Bethel, and tell you all how the Yankee campfires looked like the high Milky Way itself, all night long before the battle; how the dew silvered every sleeping soldier's face and the stacked rifles, as the dawn came up with the new day and death. And you will hug your knees and hear the wind outside going its rounds among the snowy pines, and you will listen on till the story you are hearing becomes a part of the old winds of the world and the motion of the bright stars. And probably it will take two uncles at least to carry you to bed.

A Surprise for the Teacher

SAM LEVENSON

Three days before Christmas one year when I was teaching Spanish at Tilden High School in Brooklyn, New York, there was more than the usual commotion among my students. I overheard snatches of whispered exchanges, and I gathered that a "surprise" present for the teacher was being discussed surreptitiously—and somewhat anxiously.

I didn't know how to go about discouraging the customary display of Christmas spirit I knew they couldn't afford.

Finally, uncertain myself how to begin, I asked, "All right, kids, what's up?"

There was a long silence. At last, in the rear of the classroom, a timid little girl rose. "Mr. Levenson," she began, glancing around for encouragement in her decision, "we've got a problem. . . ."

"Well, suppose you tell me about it, Gracie, and we'll see what's to be done."

Her words came pouring out. "It's your Christmas present, Mr. Levenson. We know just what we want to get you. We have it all picked out. And it's something you need. Except. . . ."

"Except?" I asked hesitantly.

"Except, Mr. Levenson, we've only been able to raise three dollars and. . . ." No one in the room moved. Gracie stared shyly at the floor and whispered, "It cost ten dollars."

I glanced around the class. All my students were sitting forward on their seats. It was a strange sight, for this was the only time during the entire term that my class gave me its undivided attention. There wasn't a face that didn't reflect Gracie's concern at the dilemma.

"Mr. Levenson," she said, "we feel very badly."

"We feel very bad," I corrected her absentmindedly.

"We hope you'll understand," she continued.

"Kids," I said, "the thought behind your gift actually means more to me than the gift itself. Your merry Christmas wishes are all . . ." I stopped in the middle of my sentence. From my desk I could see Gracie's eyes begin to fill with tears.

I couldn't find the words to discourage the class from buying its teacher a present. I rummaged through my pockets and counted out six dollars and a seventh in change. I walked over to Gracie's desk, put the money in her hand, and whispered in her ear, "You make a wonderful chairman."

Then the Christmas spirit overcame me. "Class is dismissed," I said.

After the room had emptied, I sat at my desk considering how I would raise the trolley fare to get home that evening. I had given the children my last pfennig.

Suddenly Mr. O'Hara, the principal, walked into my room, looking at me quizzically. "Mr. Levenson," he said, "as I was coming up the stairs I was nearly bowled over by a pack of wild Indians. They wouldn't by any chance be your students, would they? I didn't hear the final bell."

Sheepishly I told Mr. O'Hara the whole story of my Christmas gift. He dipped into his wallet and handed me a dollar. "Here," he said. "Treat yourself to a taxi home."

A Gift of the Heart

NORMAN VINCENT PEALE

New York City, where I live, is impressive at any time, but as Christmas approaches it's overwhelming. Store windows blaze with lights and color, furs and jewels. Golden angels, 40 feet tall, hover over Fifth Avenue. Wealth, power, opulence . . . nothing in the world can match this fabulous display.

Through the gleaming canyons, people hurry to find last-minute gifts. Money seems to be no problem. If there's a problem, it's that the recipients so often have everything they need or want that it's hard to find anything suitable, anything that will really say, "I love you."

Last December, as Christ's birthday drew near, a stranger was faced with just that problem. She had come from Switzerland to live in an American home and perfect her English. In return, she was willing to act as secretary, mind the grandchildren, do anything she was asked. She was just a girl in her late teens. Her name was Ursula.

One of the tasks her employers gave Ursula was keeping track of Christmas presents as they arrived. There were many, and all would require acknowledgment. Ursula kept a faithful record, but with a growing sense of concern. She was grateful to her American friends; she wanted to show her gratitude by giving them a Christmas present. But nothing that she could buy with her small allowance could compare with the gifts she was recording daily. Besides, even without these gifts, it seemed to her that her employers already had everything.

At night from her window Ursula could see the snowy expanse of Central Park and beyond it the jagged skyline of the city. Far below, taxis hooted and the traffic lights winked red and green. It was so different from the silent majesty of the Alps that at times she had to blink back tears of the homesickness she was careful never to show. It was in the solitude of her little room, a few days before Christmas, that her secret idea came to Ursula.

It was almost as if a voice spoke clearly, inside her head. "It's true," said the voice, "that many people in this city have much more than you do. But surely there are many who have far less. If you will think about this, you may find a solution to what's troubling you."

Ursula thought long and hard. Finally on her day off, which was Christmas Eve, she went to a large department store. She moved slowly along the crowded aisles, selecting and rejecting things in her mind. At last she bought something and had it wrapped in gaily colored paper. She went out into the gray twilight and looked helplessly around. Finally, she went up to a doorman, resplendent in blue and gold. "Excuse, please," she said in her hesitant English, "can you tell me where to find a poor street?"

"A poor street, Miss?" said the puzzled man.

"Yes, a very poor street. The poorest in the city."

The doorman looked doubtful. "Well, you might try Harlem. Or down in the Village. Or the Lower East Side, maybe."

But these names meant nothing to Ursula. She thanked the doorman and walked along, threading her way through the stream of shoppers until she came to a tall policeman. "Please," she said, "can you direct me to a very poor street in . . . in Harlem?"

The policeman looked at her sharply and shook his head. "Harlem's no place for you, Miss." And he blew his whistle and sent the traffic swirling past.

Holding her package carefully, Ursula walked on, head bowed against the sharp wind. If a street looked poorer than the one she was on, she took it. But none seemed like the slums she had heard about. Once she stopped a woman, "Please, where do the very poor people live?" But the woman gave her a stare and hurried on.

Darkness came sifting from the sky. Ursula was cold and discouraged and afraid of becoming lost.

She came to an intersection and stood forlornly on the corner. What she was trying to do suddenly seemed foolish, impulsive, absurd. Then, through the traffic's roar, she heard the cheerful tinkle of a bell. On the corner opposite, a Salvation Army man was making his traditional Christmas appeal.

At once Ursula felt better; the Salvation Army was a part of life in Switzerland too. Surely this man could tell her what she wanted to know. She waited for the light, then crossed over to him. "Can you help me? I'm looking for a baby. I have here a little present for the poorest baby I can

find." And she held up the package with the green ribbon and the gaily colored paper.

Dressed in gloves and overcoat a size too big for him, he seemed a very ordinary man. But behind his steel-rimmed glasses his eyes were kind. He looked at Ursula and stopped ringing his bell. "What sort of present?" he asked.

"A little dress. For a small, poor baby. Do you know of one?"

"Oh, yes," he said. "Of more than one, I'm afraid."

"Is it far away? I could take a taxi, maybe?"

The Salvation Army man wrinkled his forehead. Finally he said, "It's almost six o'clock. My relief will show up then. If you want to wait, and if you can afford a dollar taxi ride, I'll take you to a family in my own neighborhood who needs just about everything."

"And they have a small baby?"

"A very small baby."

"Then," said Ursula joyfully, "I wait!"

The substitute bell-ringer came. A cruising taxi slowed. In its welcome warmth, Ursula told her new friend about herself, how she came to be in New York, what she was trying to do. He listened in silence, and the taxi driver listened too. When they reached their destination, the driver said, "Take your time, Miss. I'll wait for you."

On the sidewalk, Ursula stared up at the forbidding tenement, dark, decaying, saturated with hopelessness. A gust of wind, iron-cold, stirred the refuse in the street and rattled the ashcans. "They live on the third floor," the Salvation Army man said. "Shall we go up?"

But Ursula shook her head. "They would try to thank me, and this is not from me." She pressed the package into his hand. "Take it up for me, please. Say it's from...from someone who has everything."

The taxi bore her swiftly back from dark streets to lighted ones, from misery to abundance. She tried to visualize the Salvation Army man climbing the stairs, the knock, the explanation, the package being opened, the dress on the baby. It was hard to do.

Arriving at the apartment house on Fifth Avenue where she lived, she fumbled in her purse. But the driver flicked the flag up. "No charge, Miss."

"No charge?" echoed Ursula, bewildered.

"Don't worry," the driver said. "I've been paid." He smiled at her and drove away.

Ursula was up early the next day. She set the table with special care. By the time she had finished, the family was awake, and there was all the excitement and laughter of Christmas morning. Soon the living room was a sea of gay discarded wrappings. Ursula thanked everyone for the presents she received. Finally, when there was a lull, she began to explain hesitantly why there seemed to be none from her. She told about going to the department store. She told about the Salvation Army man. She told about the taxi driver. When she finished, there was a long silence. No one seemed to trust himself to speak. "So you see," said Ursula, "I try to do a kindness in your name. And this is my Christmas present to you...."

How do I happen to know all this? I know it because ours was the home where Ursula lived. Ours was the Christmas she shared. We were like many Americans, so richly blessed that to this child from across the sea there seemed to be nothing she could add to the material things we already had. And so she offered something of far greater value: a gift of the heart, an act of kindness carried out in our name.

Strange, isn't it? A shy Swiss girl, alone in a great impersonal city. You would think that nothing she could do would affect anyone. And yet, by trying to give away love, she brought the true spirit of Christmas into our lives, the spirit of selfless giving. That was Ursula's secret—and she shared it with us all.

Christmas This Year

BOOTH TARKINGTON

Something more than a dozen years ago, at Princeton, I heard from one of the "Art Professors" that a painting by Mainardi, a fine example from the Florentine Renaissance of the high period, could be bought in New York for far less than its worth. The great Depression was then upon us; the picture had been put through an auction sale and a dealer had bid it in for a fiftieth of what had once been paid for it.

I went to his galleries; he brought out the painting and I stood puzzled before it. The central figure was that of the blonde Virgin enthroned and holding the Christ child upon her lap. That was plain enough; but who were the two tall saints flanking the throne? One, holding a book, was a woman, probably identifiable as Ste. Justina; the other one was the problem—a long, thin, elderly man, bearded, ecclesiastically robed, red-gloved and carrying four loaves of bread in token of what function I couldn't guess.

One thing was certain: this ancient gentleman was immeasurably compassionate. That was markedly his expression. A deep world sadness underlay the look of pity; he was visibly a person who suffered less his own anguish and more that of others. You saw at once that he was profoundly sorry for all of humankind.

When I had the painting on my own wall at home, I found that a gentle melancholy pervaded the room and the old saint seemed to add a wistfulness. "Don't you really wish to know who I am?" he inquired to me whenever I looked his way.

I did indeed wish to know him and to understand his sorrow, which was one of the kind we call "haunting"—all the more so because it was universal. Of all the saints, he was the one who most mourned over the miseries of this tangled world. We got out our books, wrote to iconographical experts—and lo! we had our man. The sad old saint is—Santa Claus!

He is St. Nicholas of Bari and his four loaves of bread signify his giving, his generosity. In time, as the legend grew and changed, the most jocund and hearty of all symbolic figures emerged from this acutely sad and grieving one. St. Nicholas of Bari became "Old Saint Nick," "Kriss-kringle" (a most twisted alliterative) and Santa Claus.

He, the troubled and unhappy, now comes laughing down the chimney, fat and merry, to be the jovial inspiration of our jolliest season of the year. We say that time changed him, made this metamorphosis; but it was we—"we-the-people"—who did it. Time only let us forget that St. Nicholas was a sorrowful man.

Mainardi put a date on the painting. It is clear and neat upon a step of the Virgin's throne—1507. In the long march of mankind, the four hundred and thirty-eight years that have elapsed since the Tuscan painter finished his picture is but a breath. St. Nicholas as we know him now, our jolly, shouting friend, a frolic for the children, may become the saddest of all the saints again, someday. What made us brighten him into Santa Claus was our knowledge that the world was growing kinder than it was in 1507.

St. Nicholas of Bari knew only a cruel world. Christmas of this year needs the transfigured image of him—the jolly one who is merry because the world is wise—and kind.

Susie's Letter from Santa

MARK TWAIN

Palace of St. Nicholas
In the Moon
Christmas Morning

My dear Susie Clemens:

I have received and read all the letters which you and your little sister have written me by the hand of your mother and your nurses; I have also read those which you little people have written me with your own hands—for although you did not use any characters that are in grown people's alphabet, you used the characters that all children in all lands on earth and in the twinkling stars use; and as all my subjects in the moon are children and use no characters but that, you will easily understand that I can read your and your baby sister's jagged and fantastic marks without any trouble at all. But I had trouble with those letters which you dictated through your mother and the nurses, for I am a foreigner and cannot read English writing well. You will find that I made no mistakes about the things which you and the baby ordered in your own letters—I went down your chimney at midnight when you were asleep and delivered them all myself—and kissed both of you, too, because you are good children, well trained, nice mannered, and about the most obedient little people I ever saw. But in the letter which you dictated there were some words which I could not make out for certain, and one or two small orders which I could not fill because we ran out of stock. Our last lot of kitchen furniture for dolls has just gone to a very poor little child in the North Star away up in the cold country above the Big Dipper. Your mama can show you that star and you will say: "Little Snow Flake" (for that is the child's name), "I'm glad you got that furniture, for you need it more than I." That is, you must *write* that, with your own hand, and Snow Flake will write you an answer. If you only spoke it she wouldn't hear you. Make your letter light and thin, for the distance is great and the postage very heavy.

There was a word or two in your mama's letter which I couldn't be certain of. I took it to be "a trunk full of doll's clothes." Is that it? I will call at your kitchen door about nine o'clock this morning to inquire. But I must not see anybody and I must not speak to anybody but you. When the kitchen doorbell rings, George must be blindfolded and sent to open the door. Then he must go back to the dining room or the china closet and take the cook with him. You must tell George he must walk on tiptoe and not speak—otherwise he will die someday. Then you must go up to the nursery and stand on a chair or the nurse's bed and put your ear to the speaking tube that leads down to the kitchen and when I whistle through it you must speak in the tube and say, "Welcome, Santa Claus!" Then I will ask whether it was a trunk you ordered or not. If you say it was, I shall ask you what *color* you want the trunk to be. Your mama will help you to name a

nice color and then you must tell me every single thing in detail which you want the trunk to contain. Then when I say "Good-bye and a merry Christmas to my little Susie Clemens," you must say "Good-bye, good old Santa Claus, I thank you very much and please tell that little Snow Flake I will look at her star tonight and she must look down here—I will be right in the west bay window; and every fine night I will look at her star and say, 'I know somebody up there and *like* her, too.'" Then you must go down into the library and make George close the doors that open into the main hall and everybody must keep still for a little while. Then while you are waiting I will go to the moon and get those things and in a few minutes I will come down the chimney that belongs to the fireplace that is in the hall—if it is a trunk you want—because I couldn't get such a large thing as a trunk down the nursery chimney, you know.

People may talk if they want, till they hear my footsteps in the hall. Then you tell them to keep quiet a little while until I go up the chimney. Maybe you will not hear my footsteps at all—so

you may go now and then and peep through the dining-room doors, and by and by you will see that which you want, right under the piano in the drawing room—for I shall put it there. If I should leave any snow in the hall, you must tell George to sweep it into the fireplace, for I haven't time to do such things. George must not use a broom, but a rag—or he will die someday. You watch George and don't let him run into danger. If my boot should leave a stain on the marble, George must not holystone it away. Leave it there always in memory of my visit; and whenever you look at it or show it to anybody you must let it remind you to be a good little girl. Whenever you are naughty and somebody points to that mark which your good old Santa Claus's boot made on the marble, what will you say, little sweetheart?

Good-bye for a few minutes, till I come down and ring the kitchen doorbell.

Your loving Santa Claus
Whom people sometimes call
"The Man in the Moon"

FANNIE MERRITT FARMER'S

CHRISTMAS DINNER

From *The Original Boston Cooking School Cookbook* (1896)

Menu

Clam and Oyster Soup

Bread Sticks

Olives

Celery

Salted Pecans

Roast Goose with Potato Stuffing

Apple Sauce

Cream of Lima Beans

Duchess Potatoes

Dressed Lettuce with Cheese Straws

Mince, Apple, and Squash Pies

Frozen Pudding

Vanilla Wafers

Crackers

Cheese

Café Noir

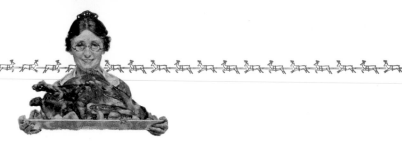

CLAM AND OYSTER SOUP

1 pint clams.	Sprig of parsley.
1 pint oysters.	Bit of bay leaf.
4 cups milk.	⅓ cup butter.
1 slice onion.	⅓ cup flour.
2 blades mace.	Salt and pepper.

Clean and pick over oysters, using one-third cup cold water; reserve liquor, and add oysters slightly chopped. Clean and pick over clams, reserve liquor, and add to hard part of clams, finely chopped; put aside soft part of clams. Heat slowly to boiling point clams and oysters with liquor from both, strain through cheese cloth. Scald milk with onion, mace, parsley, and bay leaf; remove seasonings, and add milk to stock. Thicken with butter and flour cooked together, add soft part of clams, and cook two minutes. Season with salt and pepper.

BREAD STICKS

1 cup scalded milk.	1 yeast cake dissolved in
¼ cup butter.	¼ cup lukewarm water.
1½ tablespoons sugar.	White 1 egg.
½ teaspoon salt.	3¾ cups flour.

Add butter, sugar, and salt to milk; when lukewarm, add dissolved yeast cake, white of egg well beaten, and flour. Knead, let rise, shape, let rise again, and start baking in a hot oven, reducing heat, that sticks may be crisp and dry. To shape sticks, first shape as small biscuits, roll on board (where there is no flour) with hands until eight inches in length, keeping of uniform size and rounded ends, which may be done by bringing fingers close to, but not over, ends of sticks.

APPLE SAUCE

Wipe, quarter, core, and pare eight sour apples. Make a syrup by boiling seven minutes one cup sugar and one cup water with thin shaving from rind of a lemon. Remove lemon, add enough apples to cover bottom of saucepan, watch carefully during cooking, and remove as soon as soft. Continue until all are cooked. Strain remaining syrup over apples.

CREAM OF LIMA BEANS

Soak one cup dried beans over night, drain, and cook in boiling salted water until soft; drain, add three-fourths cup cream, and season with butter and salt. Reheat before serving.

DUCHESS POTATOES

To two cups hot riced potatoes add two tablespoons butter, one-half teaspoon salt, and yolks of three eggs slightly beaten. Shape, using pastry bag and tube, in form of baskets, pyramids, crowns, leaves, roses, etc. Brush over with beaten egg diluted with one teaspoon water, and brown in a hot oven.

LETTUCE

Lettuce is obtainable all the year, and is especially valuable during the winter and spring, when other green vegetables in market command a high price. Although containing but little nutriment, it is useful for the large quantity of water and potash salts that it contains, and assists in stimulating the appetite. Curly lettuce is of less value than Tennis Ball, but makes an effective garnish.

Lettuce should be separated by removing leaves from stalk (discarding wilted outer leaves), washed, kept in cold water until crisp, drained, and so placed on a towel that water may drop from leaves. A bag made from white mosquito netting is useful for drying lettuce. Wash lettuce leaves, place in bag, and hang in lower part of icebox to drain. Wire baskets are used for the same purpose. Arrange lettuce for serving in nearly its original shape. Serve with French Dressing.

FRENCH DRESSING

½ teaspoon salt.   2 tablespoons vinegar.
¼ teaspoon pepper.   4 tablespoons olive oil.

Mix ingredients and stir until well blended. French Dressing is more easily prepared and largely used than any other dressing.

CHEESE STRAWS

Roll puff or plain paste one-fourth inch thick, sprinkle one-half with grated cheese to which has been added few grains of salt and cayenne. Fold, press edges firmly together, fold again, pat and roll out one-fourth inch thick. Sprinkle with cheese and proceed as before; repeat twice. Cut in strips five inches long and one-fourth inch wide. Bake eight minutes in hot oven. Parmesan cheese or equal parts of Parmesan and Edam cheese may be used. Cheese straws are piled log cabin fashion and served with cheese or salad course.

ROAST GOOSE WITH POTATO STUFFING

Singe, remove pinfeathers, wash and scrub a goose in hot soapsuds; then draw (which is removing inside contents). Wash in cold water and wipe. Stuff, truss, sprinkle with salt and pepper, and lay six thin strips fat salt pork over breast. Place on rack in dripping-pan, put in hot oven and bake two hours. Baste every fifteen minutes with fat in pan. Remove pork last half-hour of cooking. Place on platter, cut string, and remove string and skewers. Garnish with watercress and bright red cranberries, and place Potato Apples between pieces of watercress. Serve with Apple Sauce.

POTATO STUFFING

2 cups hot mashed potato.	⅓ cup butter.
1¼ cups soft stale bread crumbs.	1 egg.
¼ cup finely chopped fat salt pork.	1½ teaspoons salt.
1 finely chopped onion.	1 teaspoon sage.

Add to potato, bread crumbs, butter, egg, salt, and sage; then add pork and onion.

TO TRUSS A GOOSE

A goose, having short legs, is trussed differently from chicken, fowl, and turkey. After inserting skewers, wind string twice around one leg bone, then around other leg bone, having one inch space of string between legs. Draw legs with both ends of string, close to back, cross string under back, then fasten around skewers and tie in a knot.

Norman
Rockwell

PIES

Paste for pies should be one-fourth inch thick and rolled a little larger than the plate to allow for shrinking. In dividing paste for pies, allow more for upper than under crusts. Always perforate upper crusts that steam may escape. Some make a design, others pierce with a large fork.

Flat rims for pies should be cut in strips three-fourths inch wide. Under crusts should be brushed with cold water before putting on rims, and rims slightly fulled, otherwise they will shrink from edge of plate. The pastry-jagger, a simple device for cutting paste, makes rims with fluted edges.

Pies requiring two crusts sometimes have a rim between the crusts. This is mostly confined to mince pies, where there is little danger of juice escaping. Sometimes a rim is placed over upper crust. Where two pieces of paste are put together, the under piece should always be brushed with cold water, the upper piece placed over, and the two pressed lightly together; otherwise they will separate during baking.

When juicy fruit is used for filling pies, some of the juices are apt to escape during baking. As a precaution, bind with a strip of cotton cloth wrung out of cold water and cut one inch wide and long enough to encircle the plate. Squash, pumpkin, and custard pies are much less care during baking when bound. Where cooked fruits are used for filling, it is desirable to bake crusts separately. This is best accomplished by covering an inverted deep pie plate with paste and baking for under crust. Prick with a fork before baking. Slip from plate and fill. For upper crusts, roll a piece of paste a little larger than the pie plate, prick, and bake on a tin sheet.

For baking pies, perforated tin plates are used. They may be bought shallow or deep. By the use of such plates the under crust is well cooked. Pastry should be thoroughly baked and well browned. Pies require from thirty-five to forty-five minutes for baking. Never grease a pie plate; good pastry greases its own tin. Slip pies, when slightly cooled, to earthern plates.

PLAIN PASTE

1½ cups flour.	¼ cup butter.
¼ cup lard.	½ teaspoon salt.

Cold water.

Wash butter, pat, and form in circular piece. Add salt to flour, and work in lard with tips of fingers or case knife. Moisten to dough with cold water; ice

water is not an essential, but is desirable in summer. Toss on board dredged sparingly with flour, pat, and roll out; fold in butter as for puff paste, pat, and roll out. Fold so as to make three layers, turn half-way round, pat, and roll out; repeat. The pastry may be used at once; if not, fold in cheese cloth, put in covered tin, and keep in cold place, but never in direct contact with ice. Plain paste requires a moderate oven. This is superior paste and quickly made.

MINCE PIES

Mince pies should be always baked with two crusts. For Thanksgiving and Christmas pies, Puff Paste is often used for rims and upper crusts.

MINCE PIE MEAT

4 lbs. lean beef.
2 lbs. beef suet.
Baldwin apples.
3 quinces.
3 lbs. sugar.
2 cups molasses.
2 quarts cider.
4 lbs. raisins seeded
   and cut in pieces.

3 lbs. currants.
½ lb. finely cut citron.
1 quart cooking brandy.
1 tablespoon cinnamon and mace.
1 tablespoon powdered clove.
2 grated nutmegs.
1 teaspoon pepper.
Salt to taste.

Cover meat and suet with boiling water and cook until tender, cool in water in which they were cooked; the suet will rise to top, forming a cake of fat, which may be easily removed. Finely chop meat, and add it to twice the amount of finely chopped apples. The apples should be quartered, cored, and pared, previous to chopping, or skins may be left on, which is not an objection if apples are finely chopped. Add quinces finely chopped, sugar, molasses, cider, raisins, currants, and citron; also suet, and stock in which meat and suet were cooked, reduced to one and one-half cups. Heat gradually, stir occasionally, and cook slowly two hours; then add brandy and spices.

ENGLISH MINCE MEAT

5 lbs. raisins seeded.
5 lbs. suet, ⎫
5 lbs. apples, ⎬ finely
4 lbs. citron, ⎪ chopped
1½ lbs. blanched ⎭
   almonds

5 lbs. currants.
5 lbs. light brown sugar.
½ teaspoon mace.
½ teaspoon cinnamon.
2½ cups brandy.

Cook raisins, suet, apples, citron, currants, and sugar slowly for one and one-half hours; then add almonds, spices, and brandy.

SQUASH PIE

1¼ cups steamed and
   strained squash.
¼ cup sugar.
½ teaspoon salt.

¼ teaspoon cinnamon, ginger,
   nutmeg, or
½ teaspoon lemon extract.
1 egg.
⅞ cup milk.

Mix sugar, salt, and spice or extract, add squash, egg slightly beaten, and milk gradually. Bake in one crust, in quick oven at first to set rim, decrease the heat afterwards, as egg and milk in combination need to be cooked at low temperature. If a richer pie is desired, use one cup squash, one-half cup each of milk and cream, and an additional egg yolk.

APPLE PIE

4 or 5 sour apples.
⅓ cup sugar.
¼ teaspoon grated nutmeg.
   Few gratings lemon rind.

⅛ teaspoon salt.
1 teaspoon butter.
1 teaspoon lemon juice.

Line pie plate with paste. Pare, core, and cut the apples into eighths, put row around plate one-half inch from edge, and work towards centre until

plate is covered; then pile on remainder. Mix sugar, nutmeg, salt, lemon juice, and grated rind, and sprinkle over apples. Dot over with butter. Wet edges of under crust, cover with upper crust, and press edges together.

Bake forty to forty-five minutes in moderate oven. A very good pie may be made without butter, lemon juice, and grated rind. Cinnamon may be substituted for nutmeg. Evaporated apples may be used in place of fresh fruit. If used, they should be soaked over night in cold water.

FROZEN PUDDING

2½ cups milk.
1 cup sugar.
⅛ teaspoonful salt.

2 eggs.
1 cup heavy cream.
¼ cup rum.

1 cup candied fruit, cherries, pineapples, pears, and apricots.

Cut fruit in pieces, and soak several hours in brandy to cover, which prevents fruit freezing; make custard of first four ingredients; strain, cool, add cream and rum, then freeze. Fill a brick mould with alternate layers of the cream and fruit; pack in salt and ice and let stand two hours.

VANILLA WAFERS

⅓ cup butter and lard in
    equal proportions.
1 cup sugar.
1 egg.

¼ cup milk.
2½ cups flour.
2 teaspoons baking powder.
½ teaspoon salt.

2 teaspoons vanilla.

Cream the butter, add sugar, egg well beaten, milk, and vanilla. Mix and sift dry ingredients and add to first mixture. Chill thoroughly. Toss one-fourth of mixture on a floured board and roll as thinly as possible; shape with a small round cutter, first dipped in flour. Place near together on a buttered sheet and bake in a moderate oven. Gather up the trimmings and roll with another portion of dough. During rolling, the bowl containing mixture should be kept in a cool place, or it will be necessary to add more flour to dough, which makes cookies hard rather than crisp and short.